The End Is Near

and It's Going to Be

AWESOME

||||||||||||||||||||||||||||||||||||||||||||||||||||||||||||||||||||||||||||||||

The End Is Near
and It's Going to Be
AWESOME

||||||||||||||||||||||||||||||||||||||||||||||||||||||||||||||||||||||||||||||||||||||||||||||||||||||||||||||||||||||||||

How Going Broke
Will Leave America
Richer, Happier, and
More Secure

KEVIN D. WILLIAMSON

BROADSIDE BOOKS

An Imprint of HarperCollins*Publishers*

www.broadsidebooks.net

HarperCollins books may be purchased for educational, business, or sales promotional use. For information, please e-mail the Special Markets Department at SPsales@harpercollins.com.

Broadside Books™ and the Broadside logo are trademarks of HarperCollins Publishers.

FIRST EDITION

Designed by Betty Lew

Library of Congress Cataloging-in-Publication Data has been applied for.

ISBN: 978-0-06-222068-4

13 14 15 16 17   OV/RRD   10 9 8 7 6 5 4 3 2 1

For my father,

who taught me more than he knows

When the Stranger says: "What is the meaning of this city?
Do you huddle close together because you love each other?"
What will you answer? "We all dwell together
To make money from each other"? or "This is a community"?
And the Stranger will depart and return to the desert.
O my soul, be prepared for the coming of the Stranger,
Be prepared for him who knows how to ask questions.

—T. S. ELIOT, "CHORUSES FROM 'THE ROCK'"

CONTENTS

CONTENTS

iPencil

It has been said that "only God can make a tree." Why do we agree with this? Isn't it because we realize that we ourselves could not make one? Indeed, can we even describe a tree? We cannot, except in superficial terms. We can say, for instance, that a certain molecular configuration manifests itself as a tree. But what mind is there among men that could even record, let alone direct, the constant changes in molecules that transpire in the life span of a tree? Such a feat is utterly unthinkable! I, Pencil, am a complex combination of miracles: a tree, zinc, copper, graphite, and so on. But to these miracles which manifest themselves in Nature an even more extraordinary miracle has been added: the configuration of creative human energies— millions of tiny know-hows configuring naturally and spontaneously in response to human necessity and desire and in the absence of any human master-minding! Since only God can make a tree, I insist that only God could make me. Man can no more direct these millions of know-hows to bring me into being than he can put molecules together to create a tree.

—LEONARD READ, "I, PENCIL," *1958*

I hope that this book still is being read a few years from now, because my admiration for Apple's iPhone will by then seem faintly ridiculous, like Howard Wagner's enthusiasm for his new wire-recording machine in *Death of a Salesman*. From the point of view of 2013, though, the iPhone is a thing of beauty and wonder, a constant connection to much of the world's useful information, a supplementary digital brain that also allows one to make telephone calls and play Angry Birds.

In his classic essay "I, Pencil," economist Leonard Read considers the incomprehensible complexity involved in the production of a simple No. 2 pencil: the expertise in design, forestry, mining, metallurgy, engineering, transportation, support services, logistics, architecture, chemistry, machining, and other fields of knowledge necessary to create a product so common, so humble, and so cheap as to have become both ubiquitous and disposable. Read's conclusion, which is one of those fascinating truths so obvious that nobody appreciates it, is that *nobody knows how to make a pencil*. Nobody is in charge of the operation, and nobody understands it end-to-end. From the assembly-line worker to the president of the pencil company, thousands or millions of people have tiny, discrete pieces of knowledge about the process, but no coordinating authority organizes their efforts.

That is the paradox of social knowledge: Of course *we* know how to make a pencil, even though *none of us* knows how to make a pencil, and pencils get made with very little drama and no central authority, corporate or political, overseeing their creation. A mobile phone is a much more complicated thing than a No. 2 pencil, but both are the products of spontaneous order—of systems that are, in the words of the Scottish Enlightenment philosopher Adam Ferguson, the "products of human action, but not of human design."

Complex though it is, the iPhone is also a remarkably egalitarian device: The president of the United States uses one, as does the young Bengali immigrant who sold me my coffee this morning.

The iPhone lives downtown in the Financial District, and up in the South Bronx. It lives in all five boroughs of New York, in all fifty states, in Zurich and Bombay and Lagos and Buenos Aires, connecting the well-off and the not-so-well-off. It is still beyond the reach of the global poor, but it is getting more affordable and more accessible every year. It is for that reason that I have chosen this commonplace miracle as a symbol and as a benchmark against which to compare the less satisfactory features of life in the early twenty-first century. I do so in full expectation that in a few years the current iPhone will seem to us as archaic and clumsy as that gigantic Motorola cinder block that was the most coveted status symbol of Wall Street masters of the universe in the early 1980s. If you are reading this book a few years after the time of its publication, and the iPhone of 2013 seems to you hopelessly out of date, like a 1973 Ford Pinto or a videocassette recorder or a rotary-dial Bakelite telephone, then that fact will be the best evidence I can present for my argument.

The purpose of this book is to attempt to answer a question: Why is it that the telephone in my pocket gets better and cheaper every year, but many of our critical institutions grow more expensive and less effective? Why does the young Bengali immigrant have access to the same communication technology enjoyed by men of great wealth and power, but at the same time she must send her children to inferior schools, receive inferior health care, and age into an inferior retirement? And how is it that Apple can make these improvements while generating so much profit that one of its most serious corporate challenges is managing its "cash mountain"—about $100 billion at this writing, and headed toward $200 billion by some estimates—whereas government at all levels is running up enormous debts to fund stagnating or declining services?

One class of goods and services experiences regular and reliable improvements in price and quality, and that class is not limited to high-tech goods such as the iPhone. Food and clothes today represent a much smaller share of household expenses than they did a generation ago, and middle-class people have access to things that either did not exist a generation ago or were restricted to the very wealthy. A poor man today owns better shoes than a middle-class man did a few decades ago. Air travel was such a rarefied luxury good that the evocative phrase "jet set" endures even into a time in which international travel is available to the middle class, and even to the poor.

But there is another class of goods that either stagnates or follows an opposite trajectory: lower quality, higher price. These goods include education, health insurance, and many basic government services. The deterioration of these key sectors has significantly and needlessly lowered the quality of life for millions of people. Better phones and organic kale are not going to be all that useful to people whose lack of education and marketable skills is driving them toward Third World standards of living, or who are going to be bankrupted in late middle age by a dysfunctional health-care system. My analysis here will focus largely on the case of the United States, but the story is the same in many other advanced countries. There are relatively good models of politics (Switzerland, Canada, Australia), middling ones (the United States, the United Kingdom), and relatively poor ones (Mexico, India, Brazil), but dysfunction is the rule in all political enterprises, from the blue-ribbon winners to basket cases such as Venezuela or North Korea.

You are reading a book about politics, which means that you probably care about politics, which means that you almost certainly have political beliefs. Which means that at this point, the (so-called) conservatives among you will be sorely tempted to say, "Markets work, government doesn't, mystery solved!" and go back to your small business or golf game, while the (so-called) liberals among you will be sorely tempted to say, "We need to invest more resources and develop better plans. Mystery solved!" and go back to your campus office or law firm. Some of you will be tempted to say of the two major political parties, "A pox upon both your houses," and perhaps sing a hymn to nonideological pragmatism, which is of course only another form of political ideology. Each of those answers represents a major tendency in contemporary American political thought, and none of them is sufficient to our present needs.

Relatively simple political ideologies are satisfying because they are consistent and easy to assimilate into one's understanding of the world. It would not be too much to say that American politics is characterized not by two dominant political parties or philosophies but by two competing enemies lists. A master villain supports a master narrative. But a theory of everything is a theory of nothing, and theories that rely upon the dark operations of secret malice (by left-wing radicals, the Christian Right, corporations, the elites, the 1 percent, the 99 percent, the 47 percent, etc.) are inconsistent with a great many facts that are well documented and widely understood. The only real attraction that these theories can retain after even a cursory examination is their simplicity.

But life as it is actually lived is rich with incident and detail, which together form an acid in which easy generalities are dissolved. A great number of the homeless, for example, are in that condition because they suffer from severe mental disorders, often schizophrenia or a comparatively debilitating disease. Markets do not work very well for them, inasmuch as they largely lack the ability to participate in them. Government does not work very well for them, either, inasmuch as it was in many cases government that made them homeless.

Psychologists, many employed by government institutions, in the 1960s and 1970s began acting on a well-intentioned and sincerely held belief in what they called "deinstitutionalization," which, they argued, would ultimately result in the better integration of the mentally ill with the rest of society and in their living better, happier, fuller lives. This well-intentioned belief represented the professional consensus of the most prestigious experts in the field, and, when it was combined with state and local governments' desire to shift spending away from penniless (and, not coincidentally, mostly non-voting) psychotics toward taxpaying middle-class voters, it led to the shuttering of many of the institutions that had cared for the indigent mentally ill. That, not the usual bogeyman of "special interest" influence or venal corruption, is the model of what is wrong with politics.

But note: The market did not react with a solution, and neither did private charity. Our problem is not only how we *govern*, but how we *live*.

If there were self-evident solutions to such sticky problems, they probably would be implemented. Nobody wants untreated schizophrenics on the streets, and nobody profits from it. Nobody wants underperforming schools, even hard-hearted people who do not care about the students themselves—businesses profit from having highly skilled workers and consumers with disposable income, not from ignorance, unemployment, and unproductivity. Nobody wants babies suffering from phenylketonuria to go without care. There is no profit in that. The endurance of such problems suggests that there is rather more to solving them than our glib political certainties can accommodate.

In fact, we have good evidence that there is a good deal more: Jim Manzi, an entrepreneur and mathematician, examined experimental data derived from randomized field trials—the gold standard of scientific evidence—in his 2012 book, *Uncontrolled*, and his main finding was that 90 percent or more of the policy innovations in health care, education, and criminal justice produced no measureable benefit when subjected to the most rigorous standard of examination. Figuring out how to make the world better is hard. What works in theory often does not work in practice, and angrily insisting that it *should* work does not make it work.

It is possible to harness the virtues of the spontaneous orders that produced the iPhone—innovation, evolution, choice—and apply them to public problems. But a simple declaration that "markets work" is far from adequate.

What follows is neither a political manifesto nor a plan for building a utopian society. To the contrary, I will argue, among other things, that the desire to design a perfect society in theory is one of the main obstacles to achieving a better society in fact, and that the very desire to *design* human communities is itself destructive. The fundamental political problem is politics itself: not liberal politics, not conservative politics, not politics corrupted by big money or distorted by special-interest groups, but politics per se—the practice of delivering critical goods and services through the medium of federal, state, and local governments and their obsolete decision-making practices.

The good news is that the centrality of politics is a condition that is going to change, whether the political authorities are willing to accept the fact or not. The U.S. government has, for example, promised its citizens certain health-care and retirement benefits, the unfunded liabilities of which at present amount to a little more than twice the annual economic output of human civilization. Other advanced countries have made similar promises. Given that the total liabilities of the world's governments far exceed the total assets—both financial and physical—owned by the entire human race, it is very nearly a mathematical certainty that these benefits will not be paid at present value. The financial crisis of 2008–2009, the European sovereign-credit crisis that began in 2011, and the stagnation of advanced economies have shown without a doubt that, in an age of instantaneous capital flows, the sum of private economic activity is decisively more powerful than the sum of political activity.

And it isn't just for-profit economic enterprises: The day before yesterday, nobody had ever heard of WikiLeaks, and organizations such as the CIA and MI6 were held to be ruthlessly omnicompetent. But today a largely anonymous collection of online data vigilantes is powerful enough to flit about merrily making fools of the world's most powerful national-intelligence apparatuses. Individuals may use that new power wisely or irresponsibly—but they will use it, because they now have it, and soon will have more of it.

The situation is of course familiar at a more quotidian level: Millions of Americans working in cash-based, tip-dependent service jobs radically underreport their incomes for tax purposes. Among waitresses and bartenders, tax evasion is a social norm, not an exception, but it would be impractical if not impossible to really crack down on them all, in spite of the inquisitional powers enjoyed by the soft-spoken Torquemadas of the IRS. The very wealthy have legal and extralegal methods for evading taxes as well: Both Bain Capital and *Gawker*, one of its angriest critics, divert a great deal of money to shell corporations based in the Cayman Islands, while a fair number of celebrities and heirs domicile themselves in Switzerland, and General Electric's internal legal staff is known half-jokingly as the world's most prestigious tax-law firm, enabling the blue-chip company to pay no corporate income taxes at all in some years.

But what happens when it is not only the very rich and low-wage service workers who start evading taxes? Technology, including privacy technology and financial innovation, is increasingly giving the broad middle class the same power to dodge taxes once reserved to the billionaires and bartenders. Milton Friedman, the Nobel laureate economist, presciently observed that the biggest social change to come out of the invention of the Internet may be to make it much more difficult for governments to collect taxes and regulate labor. For better and for worse, it already has made it more difficult for government to keep secrets, to censor dissenters, or to enforce laws against things like marijuana, prostitution, and off-the-books work for people ranging from gardeners to copywriters and graphic designers. The concentrated power of the FBI and the nation's police departments is simply insufficient to police all of Craigslist or Backpage.com. Innovations such as private currencies began on the black and gray markets but are slowly working their way into the mainstream.

Meanwhile, government's traditional partner—the modern shareholder corporation—is in decline as well. The size of the average corporation has been shrinking since 1975 as technology-enabled competition and outsourcing have led to increasing specialization. The ever-more-precise division of labor means that Apple designs and sells iPhones but does not manufacture them, while Foxconn and other Apple partners may manufacture products but may not design or sell them. A generation ago, most firms had their own payroll, human resources, and tax departments; new corporations such as Paychex have emerged to take on those tasks that are not part of a firm's core business. The size of firms has declined, but the number involved in specialized business processes has grown.

Unprecedented fiscal pressure on overleveraged governments,

the increasing mobility of people and capital, the decline of the traditional integrated corporation as a model of production, the increasing power of privacy technology and financial innovation: All of these together are in the process of changing the relationship between the individual and the state—in the right direction. The end is near, and it's going to be awesome . . . if we get it right.

Building the institutions of a more humane society to pick up where the twentieth-century centralized state left off is not going to be easy, and the way forward is far from self-evident. But doing so requires that we understand that there are more possible destinations before us than offered by the traditional left/right/regulator/ deregulator political map. Our political language has constrained our political thinking, and too often we argue as though our only choices were to be found in one of two dark imaginations: that of Thomas Hobbes or that of Ayn Rand, the all-powerful Leviathan or an atomistic individualism that denies the social nature of *Homo sapiens*. Neither of those visions is consistent with twenty-first-century life: Neither Hobbes's false choice between utter chaos and utter servitude nor Rand's romantic egoism accounts for the complexity of human life.

It has long been observed that while historians date the fall of the Roman Empire to A.D. 376, the imperial implosion would have been news to Roman authorities and Roman subjects for a century after that—the empire didn't know that it had fallen. (Politicians: *always* the last to know.) A similar dynamic is at work today: The edifice of government looks as imposing as ever, perhaps more so. But something has changed. Sobering as it is, the collective debt of the world's governments is an indicator not only of their aggregate fiscal irresponsibility but of a much deeper trend that is becoming manifest as the deficiencies of the political model play themselves out. The model of organizing community life that has prevailed since the late eighteenth century is in the process of disintegrating. That fact is the *good* news. The *bad* news is that politics is not going to go quietly, and the political class may make the coming changes unnecessarily painful and disruptive. The historic challenge of our time is to anticipate as best we can the coming changes and to begin developing alternative institutions and social practices to ensure the continuation of a society that is humane, secure, free, and prosperous. In confronting this problem, it is important that we resist the urge to cling to naïve simplification, and that we understand our institutions and conditions as they *are*, not as they *should be*; as they were *intended to be*, and certainly not as we *wish they were*.

With apologies to the sainted Thomas Jefferson, there are few if any truths that we may hold to be self-evident. The words of the Declaration of Independence are both beautiful and inspiring, but to believe that we may find within them the answers to our present difficulties is to be a hostage to sentimentality. The Declaration of Independence is a statement of our aspirations, not a description of our reality. Good poetry makes bad politics.

What makes good politics? The question itself is a problem, because to ask the question assumes that good politics is possible. It is not, and the main reason for that is not ethical but technical: Political rhetoric aside, politics as an institution fails first and foremost because it cannot manage the complex processes of modern life, because doing so would require politicians to be able to gather and process amounts of information so vast that they are literally incalculable. Second, politics fails because people do not cease to be self-interested economic actors once elected to political office or hired by a government agency; the profit-maximizing forces that operate in the marketplace operate in politics, too, whether "profit" is measured in conventional economic terms or in power, prestige, or some other commodity. The first two factors are compounded by an inescapable third shortcoming of the political model: Unlike practically every other institution in human society, politics cannot *learn*— because it cannot *evolve*. In biological terms, the operative mechanism of evolution is, not to put too fine a point on it, *death*. Species evolve because death sorts out the reproductive success of individual members of that species. (That is an observation about the facts of biology, not a prescription for a public policy of Social Darwinism, a creed that—to the extent it ever actually existed—drew precisely the wrong conclusion from evolution.) Human beings evolve socially as well as biologically as old models of individual and community life are displaced by new models more suited to present conditions. The band of hunters becomes the trading-post village becomes the city-state becomes the Swiss federation, and skill with software design displaces skill wielding a spear. Industries and economic arrangements evolve through the bankruptcy and dissolution of individual firms and production models. Science evolves when hypotheses are driven to extinction by new and better hypotheses. If it were not for death at the individual level, species would not evolve. If it were not for the dissolution of failed enterprises (for-profit or nonprofit), economic arrangements would not evolve. But politics does not die. Politics is the Immortal Corporation.

CHAPTER 1

The Immortal Corporation

Everything simple is false. Everything complex is unusable.

—PAUL VALÉRY

The United States Steel Corporation was built to last—forever. Formed by the union of J. P. Morgan's financial empire and Andrew Carnegie's consolidated steel interests, it was the first corporation in the world to have a market value in excess of $1 billion. Carnegie took his payment—the equivalent of $6 billion in contemporary dollars—in the form of fifty-year gold bonds, which took up so much room that the bank in which they were deposited had to build a special vault to house them. The new company was worth about 4.5 percent of the gross domestic product of the United States—proportionally far larger than any contemporary corporation. But it was an enterprise that would be unfamiliar to the modern businessman or investor: Morgan, the archcapitalist, had a vision of the role of industry that was in many ways similar to that of such anticapitalist thinkers as the socialist economist Enrico Barone and the American fascist intellectual Lawrence Dennis: unitary, rational, monopolistic, centrally planned, and tightly aligned with government. Morgan of course was interested in profit as well, something Barone and Dennis would have constrained, but his abhorrence of "wasteful competition" and his faith in centrally directed economic endeavor were very much of a piece with the progressive thinking of his time, even if that fact would have been invisible (and shocking) to Morgan and his critics. Morgan and many of his tycoon contemporaries regarded themselves as men of practical intelligence who could cast their expert gaze across the economic landscape and accurately judge what the nation needed: railroads here, steel mills there, factories here, working hand in glove with government to achieve those goals.

Though they held no elected offices, they were in a very real sense *politicians* as much as businessmen. The lines between those two occupations would become ever more indistinct: In the 1950s, secretary of defense and former General Motors president Charles Erwin Wilson was derided for his belief that "what was good for the country was good for GM, and vice versa" (almost always misquoted as "What is good for GM is good for America"), but the 2008 bailout of GM and the remarkable celebration of that policy at the 2012 Democratic National Convention suggest that the idea is very much alive. Morgan, Carnegie, and their associates were in an important way forerunners of what would later come to be known as *corporatism*, the proponents of which hold that a close alliance between industrial interests and government could be forged in order to rationally serve the public good, that is, to ensure that what is good for GM is in fact good for America. Morgan's new company's name, then, was well chosen: It was to be *the* U.S. Steel Corporation.

But it did not turn out that way, and that's a good thing. Today, U.S. Steel is only a division of another larger company, employing a fraction of the workers it once did. The world economy and its appetite for steel have grown enormously since U.S. Steel was founded, but today the company produces only about as much steel as it did in 1902.

B ig Business isn't what it used to be.

Twenty-first-century corporations are more like temporary associations of people and capital lucky to survive for a few decades, and, if present trends continue, the future corporation will be an even more ad hoc tissue of tenuous short-term relationships. It is impossible to imagine Facebook's growing into something like *Blade Runner*'s mighty Tyrell Corporation—indeed, many analysts do not expect the firm to outlive its much-hyped initial stock offering by very many years. Given the power of branding and the impressive headquarters that corporations still sometimes inhabit, and American presidents' habit of picking corporate executives for influential positions, it is easy to mistake familiar corporations for enduring, deeply structured enterprises. The illusion of permanence that led to the building of such monumental structures as the Chrysler Building is for the most part a thing of the past—which is why there are multibillion-dollar corporations that work out of rented space. Nobody is going to be issuing any gold-backed fifty-year corporate bonds and building special vaults to house them when most firms will not be around for much more than a decade. In truth, a successful twenty-first-century corporation is really more like an unusually enjoyable dinner party: a happy coincidence that is in part the product of careful forethought and execution, but also the product of the spontaneous interactions among people and events. An important difference between the early twentieth century and the early twenty-first century is that businesses have become more specialized and the division of labor radically more precise, so the corporate life cycle runs more quickly. The corporate lifetime is shortening because the pace of social learning is accelerating. More complex economic entities develop adaptive strategies more quickly. We recognize our economic mistakes more quickly and develop alternatives in great number and at high speed. Understood properly, bankruptcy and business failure are pedagogical tools: They are an important part of how individuals, businesses, and industries learn—and the global marketplace is an exercise in collective social learning.

Strange thing: Nobody ever stopped to ask, "If there is no U.S. Steel, then where will we get steel?"

The vulnerability of individual enterprises is a consequence of the radical improvements in productive economic activity as a whole. U.S. Steel declined because the standard of living in the United States and elsewhere was rising. Between 1960 and the turn of the century, real steel prices fell by about half, while the quality of steel improved significantly. We often see only the unpleasant side of such developments: the laid-off workers, the shuttered mills, the declining steel towns. Those are very powerful images because they are discrete and specific. The pain is concentrated, but the benefits are widely dispersed. But if you understand that the purpose of the steel industry is to provide steel to people who need steel, then the story of the industry over the past century has been one of remarkable success—it is only a failure from the political point of view. What is more difficult to see but ultimately more important is that tens of millions of enterprises and projects in the United States and around the world benefited from access to better and less expensive steel: Contractors building skyscrapers benefited, companies building cars benefited, people living in houses and apartment buildings benefited—everybody who uses steel benefited, which as a practical matter means everybody benefited. The decline of U.S. Steel (and of U.S. steel) is a tragedy only if you believe that the purpose of the steel industry is to provide high-wage jobs in Pittsburgh. But jobs are a means, not an end. As the economists John Papola and Russ Roberts point out, we could easily achieve permanent full employment by drafting the entire population into the military, but as a result we'd all starve to death.

Politics is choking to death on its own contradictions because it cannot evolve. Imagine a world in which U.S. Steel and other firms could not as a practical matter fail, as in the case of government-chartered monopolies. U.S. Steel in its prime was the product of an improved business model that displaced older, less efficient competitors. Without the pressure and opportunity created by the possibility of failure, the U.S. steel industry—and the entire U.S. economy—would be (at best) stuck in the early nineteenth century. It seems paradoxical, but failure is what makes us rich. (And we are, even in these troubled times, fabulously rich.) We'd all be a lot worse off if corporations such as U.S. Steel did in fact live forever. Obvious counterexamples include Amtrak and the U.S. Postal Service, two institutions that would have failed long ago if not for government support—subsidies for Amtrak, the government-chartered monopoly on letter delivery for the postal service. The cost of their corporate immortality is not only the waste associated with maintaining them, but the fact that their continued existence prevents the emergence of superior alternatives. No death, no evolution. A political establishment is a near-deathless thing: Even after the bitter campaign of 2012, voters returned essentially the same cast of characters to Washington, virtually ensuring the continuation of the policies with which some 90 percent of voters pronounced themselves dissatisfied. Politics endures, but human action evolves. We learn.

And what are we learning? How to take care of one another, which is the point of what we sometimes call *capitalism*. (Don't tell Ayn Rand.)

It is remarkable that we speak and think about commerce as though *competitiveness* were its most important feature. There is, as noted, a certain Darwinian aspect to economic competition—and of course we humans do in fact compete over scarce resources. But what is remarkable about human action is not its *competitiveness* but its almost limitless *cooperativeness*. Competition is only one of the ways that we learn how best to cooperate with one another—competition is a *means* to the higher *end* of social cooperation. Cooperation exists elsewhere in the animal kingdom, but we human beings cooperate on a species-wide, planetary level, which is a relatively new development in our evolution, the consequences of which we have not yet fully appreciated. If you consider the relationship of the organism to its constituent organs, the relationship of the organ to its cells, or the relationship of the single cell to its organelles, it would not be an overstatement to say that the division of labor is the essence of life itself: Birds do it, bees do it, but human beings do it better. The size and complexity of our brains evolved in parallel to the size and complexity of our social groups. The argument for cooperative human action is not just economics, but biology. Our social institutions are just as much a product of evolutionary processes as our bodies are. And it is through our social institutions, not through our individual brains, that we learn to deal with the problem of *complexity*.

Thus, we do not have *the* U.S. Steel Corporation, a tightly integrated and hierarchical operation overseen by a CEO with an omniscient command of his operation. We have lots of U.S. steel corporations, and a worldwide steel industry, and many worldwide industries making products that are substitutes for steel, from aluminum to carbon fiber to nanotubes. It would be difficult to argue that anybody would be better off if we had only *the* U.S. Steel Corporation—anybody except U.S. Steel's shareholders and employees, that is. But we do have *the* U.S. Postal Service, *the* Social Security Administration, and *the* local government-school monopoly in your hometown. These agencies underperform consistently when compared against such benchmarks of innovation as the software industry or the biotech industry. They fail because they attempt to substitute a single brain, or a relatively small panel of brains organized into a bureaucracy, for the collective cognitive firepower of millions or billions of people. Put simply, they attempt to manage systems that are too complex for them to understand.

For all the debates about teaching evolution in the public schools or evaluating data about climate change, it is here that political practice is most radically at odds with scientific understanding. Complexity is a specialized scientific field dedicated to attempting to understand extremely complicated phenomena, for instance the question of how the electrochemical reactions in the three-pound ball of meat known as the human brain produce consciousness. We know a great deal about neurons and their workings, about the anatomy of the brain and the relationships among its various areas. Entire academic careers have been spent studying the most minute details imaginable about the brain. But if you ask a scientist how close he thinks we are to being able to put those pieces together into a model of how human consciousness works, he is likely to point out to you that we still aren't very good at predicting the weather more than a week out. Complexity is humbling, but politics is immune to humility. That is not just a shortcoming of virtue, but a real practical problem.

Take, for example, the problem of designing a national health-care system. Washington is packed to the gills with people who believe that they have the ability to design an intelligent national health-care system, but there is not one who does—no Democrat, no Republican, no independent. The information burden is just too vast. Imagine a radically simplified health-care system, one in which any medical problem could be treated by taking one of fifty pills, but you can have only one pill a month, so you have to prioritize. That presents each individual with 58,150,627,116,341,760,000 options (that's "58 quintillion")—the number of ways to rank 12 choices out of 50 options—and political managers would have to do so for every American. Since there are 300 million Americans, we have to do a calculation for each one, meaning that we have to consider 1.74×10^{28} options, one of those numbers so large that we don't have a common name for it. And since we'll assume that people's needs will change over time (an eighteen-year-old doesn't have the same health-care needs as an eighty-one-year-old), we'll want to review everybody's plan once a year. As they say in the political speeches, we're going to consider *all of our options* and take *all of the information* into account.

Except we pretty obviously aren't.

Imagine for the purposes of our thought experiment that we are highly dedicated servants of the public weal, armed with vast arrays of supercomputers able to condense the complexity of individual lives down into a simplified mathematical algorithm. As public servants go, we are one part Gandhi and two parts Einstein—top-drawer, righteous political stuff. We are so good at this that we can scan every American's data and in one second compare that data against one of our underlying distributions of possible health-care choices. But as heroic as that effort is, it leaves us with a problem: We have 1.74×10^{28} options to compare against the needs of the American people, and even at a rate of one scenario per second we're in big trouble, since the number of seconds that have passed since the beginning of the universe (dated from the Big Bang, some 14 billion years ago) is a lot less than the number of possibilities we have to consider, only 4.42×10^{17} seconds in total. Put in perspective, the number of options to be examined in our ridiculously *simplified* system is 30 billion times the number of seconds that have passed since the beginning of time. Even if we could imagine a situation in which we could radically simplify human needs such that we could examine one possible outcome each second, we still have an impossible calculation in front of us.

In the real world, the complexity here gets pretty hairy pretty quickly: There's a lot more to health care than picking any 12 of 50 options out of a hat and ranking them. There are hundreds or thousands of factors that go into relatively simple things such as infertility therapy, and of course many of our pressing health-care concerns—cancer, HIV, obesity—far exceed the limits of our medical knowledge, entangling us in questions related to genetics, human behavior, environmental factors, and dozens of intractable realms of inquiry that are both far afield from our specific medical concerns and yet critical to actually understanding them. This is no No. 2 pencil, and not even an iPhone—this is complexity in one of its fullest human expressions.

The hubris of the political-planning conceit commanded the attention of, among others, two Austrian economists, Ludwig von Mises and F. A. Hayek. Mises argued that under central planning, economic calculation never actually happened because it became de facto impossible—information is dispersed throughout the marketplace, central planners have no way of gathering information about people's real preferences, and in any event the sheer volume of data necessary to the task meant that calculation never happened. Rational economic planning, he concluded, was impossible, because the planners could never process sufficient information to make rational calculations. Whatever their plans were based on, he argued, we could be sure that the central planners were *not* "considering all the options" and "taking into account all of the information."

He called this the "socialist calculation problem," but its application is hardly limited to forms of government that are either explicitly or implicitly socialist. In fact, the calculation problem constrains all economic activity outside of those in which knowledge is dispersed among a large number of cooperating agents—that, not corruption or negligence, is what probably best explains the gross misallocation of material resources one sees in even the most traditional of governmental undertakings, such as law enforcement and the military. Needless to say, these objections to central planning were not only ignored but in some cases actively suppressed: Professor F. A. Harper was driven out of Cornell University for assigning Hayek's *Road to Serfdom* to his students—such reactionary criticism of national central-planning ambitions was considered beyond the pale of respectable public discourse.

Because of the knowledge problem, there is an inevitable discontinuity between political plans and reality. It is no accident that big political ideas often are referred to as "road maps"—think of Paul Ryan's long-term fiscal "road map" or Barack Obama's "road map to recovery" or the 2002 "road map for peace" in the Israeli-Palestinian conflict. Maps are by their nature simplifications—maps are models.

Many fields of study understand that they are simplifying reality and allow that at times they must make an inevitable trade-off between accuracy and usability. E. O. Wilson acknowledged that when he said that he and his fellow scholars of evolution "deliberately try to simplify the natural universe in order to produce mathematical principles. . . . We don't even try to take all the possible factors in a particular situation into account, such as sudden changes of weather or the effects of unusual tides." Classical economics describes abstract economic forces, not human life as lived. Economic models are extremely useful tools, but they have important limitations as well. There is a critical difference between using simplified models to try to *understand* what has happened and why, versus trying to use models to *make things happen* in a complex human society (or even in a simple human society, or in an ant society).

Complexity science shows us that we remain very far from understanding certain intricate phenomena. More important, it also suggests hard real-world limitations on our ability to know certain things about complex systems. Isaac Newton's clockwork universe was predictable: Understand the mechanics of the parts and you understand the mechanics of the whole. Pierre-Simon Laplace took this reductive view to its natural conclusion when he wrote: "We may regard the present state of the universe as the effect of its past and the cause of its future. An intellect which at a certain moment would know all forces that set nature in motion, and all positions of all items of which nature is composed, if this intellect were also vast enough to submit these data to analysis, it would embrace in a single formula the movements of the greatest bodies of the universe and those of the tiniest atom; for such an intellect, nothing would be uncertain, and the future just like the past would be present before its eyes." Laplace sought only to establish as a matter of logic that to understand the universe as a whole is possible *in principle*. With the advent of electronic computing, some wondered if creating some version of Laplace's all-knowing brain (known in the scientific literature as "Laplace's demon") might not be possible *in fact* as well as in principle. In the Soviet Union, the strange amalgamation of computer science and Marxist ideology known as "cybernetics" took seriously the proposition that computer simulations could be used not only to produce perfect five-year economic plans but also to organize all of human social life. It certainly is an attractive proposition: a single, godlike intelligence watching the gears of the universe turn in perfect synchronization, a place for everything and everything in its place. It is no wonder that Laplace, facetiously asked about the role of God in his model of the universe, replied: "I have no need of that hypothesis." Of course he didn't. Marx didn't, either, for precisely the same reason: If the universe can be modeled in principle, everything else is only an exercise in engineering. It is no accident that Marx's epigones called their system "scientific socialism." But reality turns out to be more tangled up than even the remarkable minds of Newton, Laplace, and Marx had imagined. Chaotic systems are sometimes predictable—and, conversely, chaos sometimes arises out of relatively simple and orderly systems without outside intervention. As Melanie Mitchell of Portland State University puts it in her magisterial *Complexity*, "The behavior of some simple, deterministic systems can be impossible, *even in principle*, to predict in the long term." There are very few straight paths in the universe, but an endless supply of random walks.

Social systems are neither simple nor deterministic. Ant colonies and beehives do unpredictable things. Social systems involving human beings, who have a remarkable tendency to bounce around the planet (and occasionally beyond) in the most unpredictable fashion, are many orders of magnitude more complex than are insect societies. They should inspire commensurate humility not only in those who would seek to understand them but also and especially in those who would seek to rule them. There is no Laplace's demon among the 435 members of the House, one hundred senators, nine justices of the Supreme Court, or single president, each and every one of whom presumes to command the knowledge necessary to shape the affairs of the United States. Complexity theorists have not, as of this writing, even agreed upon how to measure the complexity of a system as complex as the division of labor that produces No. 2 pencils, let alone health-care systems or financial markets. These types of systems exhibit complexity so vast that it is literally immeasurable, even in principle, a fact that has important consequences for politics, the practitioners of which go about studiously not thinking about the depth of their aggregate ignorance, which is of course the inverse of the aggregate complexity depth of the systems they pretend to manage. Immeasurable complexity, immeasurable ignorance: Perhaps that state of affairs will change, but there is at present little reason to expect it to.

So, how do private companies know what to produce for public use without some Laplace's demon telling them what to do and when to do it? How do we learn how to cooperate? As Read noted about his beloved No. 2 pencil, nobody is in charge of the process, which is the result of a spontaneous order. The CEO of the pencil company understands only a small part of how his business works, and the pencil company collectively understands only a small part of the process. The system works because the underlying spontaneous order, even though its vast complexity is beyond our understanding, has a built-in mechanism for getting less wrong over time, mostly through trial and error—which is to say, mostly through failure. It is a form of social evolution that is metaphorically parallel to biological evolution. Consider the case of New Coke, or Betamax, or McDonald's Arch Deluxe, or Clairol's Touch of Yogurt Shampoo (which is something that, I hasten to add, actually *existed*): When hordes of people don't show up to buy the product, then the product dies.

Like a bee swarm choosing the wrong tree, choosing the wrong formula for Coke results in extinction—in this case commercial extinction rather than biological extinction. Every practicing scientist expects to spend his life producing hypotheses that will in almost every case fail when put to experimental evaluation. McDonald's as a matter of ordinary business has put out scores of products destined to fail in the laboratory of the marketplace. As with many healthy enterprises, the corporate culture of McDonald's is such that there is no penalty attached to the failure of a new product; McDonald's expects that many of its deliciously ass-fattening innovations will fail. McDonald's knows that it is engaged in a process of trial and error, which is to say a process of experimentation. Other firms, Capital One notable among them, have developed programs of explicit experimentation. Looked at with fresh eyes, McDonald's is science, its restaurants are laboratories, and that Happy Meal on the table in front of you, like the iPhone in your pocket, is a product of evolution, highly refined by countless tiny revisions through dozens of iterations moving toward a more perfect expression of its ineffable Happy Meal ethos—by no means moving in a straight line, but guided by the gift of failure in the direction of *less wrong.* Over time, less wrong looks pretty good: Look in your pocket. Look in the mirror: You're a big improvement on *Homo erectus.*

Apple may not know exactly how the iPhone is doing vis-à-vis all of its competitors around the world at any given moment, but it has an excellent idea of whether its products are getting more profitable or less profitable, and a pretty solid idea of whether its competitors' products are getting more profitable or less profitable. It has its own internal accounts and financial analysis, and it also has microsecond-by-microsecond guidance from the stock market, where millions of people are constantly engaged in analyzing every aspect of Apple's business and that of its competitors, for their own reasons, and then voting with their investments about whether the firms are moving in the right direction or the wrong one. Apple doesn't always get it right—remember the Newton?—but it does consistently get less wrong.

The problem of politics is that it does not know how to get less wrong. It is as a practical matter impossible to design a national health-care policy that can be tweaked and improved every quarter, or on-the-fly in real time as problems are discovered, as software is. It is nearly impossible to imagine political institutions creating something like a software-update feature for Social Security or the War on Drugs. Resistance to innovation is a part of the deep structure of politics. In that, it is like any other monopoly. It never goes out of business—despite flooding the market with defective and dangerous products, mistreating its customers, degrading the environment, cooking the books, and engaging in financial shenanigans that would have made Gordon Gekko pale to contemplate.

Politics is a kind of island in the evolutionary stream—isolated, unchanging, incapable of learning because it is insulated against going extinct. Politics is the last monopoly, the Immortal Corporation. You'll never see a capitol building with a GOING OUT OF BUSINESS sign hanging out front—even genuinely bankrupt, undeniably insolvent political regimes from Argentina to Greece for the most part go on about their business, even after defaulting on their financial obligations. If the bees in a particular hive make a bad decision about relocating to a new tree, those bees die, and if enough members of a species make similarly poor decisions, that species goes extinct. Consumer products follow a very similar pattern. And if a firm offers enough bad products or makes a sufficient number of bad financial decisions, it vanishes, too (unless it is a politically connected Wall Street bank or an influential manufacturing concern—more about that later). Firms learn from their mistakes and from the mistakes of others. And, like individual human beings, they learn by copying more successful efforts. Individual companies come and go, entire industries rise and fall, but the store of knowledge embedded in our aggregate economic practices continues to grow and to become ever more refined: We really do know how to make much better cars, telephones, and refrigerators than we did in 1960. But we do not have better politics. And *politics* here means both the formal structures of government and those nongovernmental institutions closely enmeshed with them, for example, the ethanol industry, which is a private, for-profit enterprise that by the industry's own account simply would not exist without a federal mandate that all gasoline contain a minimum percentage of ethanol in the blend. Government-supported firms such as General Motors and General Electric are properly considered part of politics, as are the specific operations of other private firms that operate through the power of government, for example, Lockheed Martin's defense-contracting wing.

The temptation here again is to oversimplify and conclude that profit-seeking enterprises working in a free market work while political bureaucracies fail. But that does not capture the truth of our situation. The radical advances in quality of life that have characterized human society since the Industrial Revolution are by no means limited to profit-seeking enterprises: There was nothing like Wikipedia even a few years ago, and that extraordinarily valuable collection of knowledge was assembled independent of the profit motive. The major factor contributing to evolution of goods and services is the social learning that occurs as a result of iterative, evolutionary processes.

That learning radically reduces the transaction costs associated with cooperative enterprises. The people who contribute to Wikipedia have little or no conventional profit-oriented motive for methodically working to improve one another's work, yet they've discovered that the value of cooperating is greater than the cost, even when the effort is evaluated in terms that are not strictly economic. The same forces create an incentive for cooperation among traditional profit-seeking enterprises. For example, banks, car loan companies, and other consumer finance businesses universally share consumer credit information across the industry at considerable cost to themselves, even though each individual bank would be better off simply cutting off its bad-risk borrowers in the hope that they would go down the street to a competitor and cause them losses. Gas drilling companies jointly develop environmental best-practices models substantially in excess of what they are legally required to do by their regulators, even though doing so imposes costs on the cooperating firms and confers a competitive economic advantage on non-cooperating firms.

Consider that our most successful social institution is, almost without question, science. From a narrowly profit-seeking point of view, scientists would have a very strong incentive to hoard knowledge and keep their findings secret; in reality, scientific practice is precisely the opposite: Scientific knowledge is held to have more value as it is more widely disseminated. And while there certainly are commercial aspects to scientific research, the gold standard of scientific knowledge comes not from market assessments and prof-itability but from peer review and repeat experimentation. In each case we see important growth in the stock of intellectual capital to the competitive economic advantage of no individual party—but at great advantage to the common good.

The scientific method and market processes in many impor-tant ways resemble one another, being based on hypothesis, trial-and-error experimentation, and third-party evaluation. Most new products and new businesses fail, and most new scientific hypoth-eses turn out to be wrong. There is no shame in being wrong, and even the most successful operators in those fields make significant mistakes. The problem is not being wrong but rather persisting in wrongness—failing to get *less wrong* over time. Scientists and entre-preneurs may be individually arrogant, but both of their underly-ing models of operation depend upon openness to discovering that one's beliefs are wrong and taking action to correct them. Virgin Group founder Richard Branson describes his greatest failure in business as refusing to accept that his beloved chain of music stores was no longer a viable business model in the age of downloading—a failure, in short, of humility.

Humility is not only a private virtue—it is a *social technology*. By keeping in mind that we may be wrong—that we are in fact very likely to be wrong in important ways—we help each other and our-selves to become *less wrong* over time. In animals, there are bio-logical mechanisms to allow that to happen. Without being open to the possibility that one is wrong—and not just trivially wrong, but wrong in some fundamental and important way—it is impos-sible to learn, to get *less wrong*. Ideas, like genes, cultural habits, and tastes, are transmitted through interacting populations. "Thought is an infection," Wallace Stevens once observed, "and in the case of certain thoughts it becomes an epidemic." Scientists learn from one another in a formal way, but our ability to learn from one another need not follow any rigorous protocol—or even be conscious. What is important is that we create conditions for experiment and failure, which is what leads to learning.

Politics, almost alone among our contemporary institutions, lacks a strong and reliable evolutionary feedback mechanism to help it learn. In theory, public debate and the democratic process are supposed to help politics to learn and evolve in the way that non-political institutions do, but in practice these institutions are not nearly robust enough to accommodate the complexity of contemporary life in highly developed, modern technological civilizations. One reason for that is that political goods are bundled and impossible to disaggregate. In normal market processes, we have limited interaction with any given firm: We may buy our telephones and computers from Apple, but we buy our cars from somebody else, finance our mortgages with another company, buy our food from yet another company, our medicines from yet another, etc. We have dozens or hundreds of firms to choose from when it comes to most products, and we buy thousands of products, meaning that the possible number of different consumer-provider relationships we could choose to have is truly astronomical, a number with hundreds of zeros at the end of it. To make matters even more complex, we routinely change our minds about which providers we prefer: Sometimes we go to Whole Foods, sometimes we go to Trader Joe's. Both consumers and producers react to these ever-shifting relationships, constantly changing the mix of products, features, and prices in response to one another's actions. That is how social learning happens in the marketplace. It works because there are lots of players (billions of producers and consumers) and lots of repeated interaction.

Imagine if we had to sign a contract to buy everything—food, shelter, clothes, medicine, Angry Birds—from one company, and we only had two companies from which to choose. And worse, those two companies were something like cell phone providers: We have to sign multiyear contracts that are expensive or impossible to get out of. The providers would not only have less incentive to figure out how to best serve our needs, but—more important—they would also have less *ability* to do so: There would be much less rich interaction with consumers, fewer competitors to learn from, fewer successful innovations to copy, and in general a good deal less social learning going on. Even if the two companies constituting this duopoly were nonprofit enterprises run by brilliant and saintly executives, they would not do nearly as good a job of taking care of their customers as would a normal marketplace with lots of competing firms doing lots of different things. Which is to say: They would look precisely like our democratic political system.

As Hayek observed: "Even if railways, road and air transport, or the supply of gas and electricity were all inevitably monopolies, the consumer is unquestionably in a much stronger position so long as they remain separate monopolies than when they are 'coordinated' by a central control. Private monopoly is scarcely ever complete and even more rarely of long duration or able to disregard potential competition. But a state monopoly is always a state-protected monopoly—protected against both potential competition and effective criticism. It means in most instances that a temporary monopoly is given the power to secure its position for all time—a power almost certain to be used."

The inescapable problem of politics is that political methods lack sufficient feedback loops allowing institutions to become less wrong over time: Once you've built that six-lane superhighway connecting

Canyon, Texas (population 13,570) with Tucumcari, New Mexico (population 5,354), it's there, and when it fails to deliver the promised economic benefits but does deliver a great deal of sprawl and blight, you cannot as a practical matter unbuild it. The 1967 Ford Mustang was a tremendous car—but, strangely enough, nobody is building new ones. Great things are no less great for being for a particular place and a particular time. Politics aspires to permanence. You don't get a new 1968 model superhighway once you've figured out the bugs in the 1967 model. Other than Social Security, there are very few 1935-vintage products still in use.

It is for this reason—monopolistic characteristics, aspiration to permanence, to fixed final states—that political institutions continue to be dysfunctional, even when they are staffed by good and intelligent people. To put it simply, being wrong in politics doesn't hurt enough. There is a price to pay for being wrong in politics, but the effects are widely dispersed and time-delayed. And the pain of being wrong in politics is likely to fall on somebody other than the politician. Partly this insulation is by design: You may be confident that you will never meet a U.S. senator who lives in a federal housing project, earns the federal minimum wage, or relies upon Social Security for his retirement income. What holds true at the national level holds true at the local level: About 40 percent of the public school teachers in Chicago send their own children to private schools, insulating their families from the effects of political policies for which the teachers themselves are in no small part responsible through the political actions of their union. Police officers tend to keep guns at home for self-defense rather than rely upon the officers of any particular shift to protect them and their families. Timothy Geithner, who as Treasury secretary had final authority over the Internal Revenue Service, famously didn't pay his taxes. Politicians are always building utopias, but the curious thing is that none of them wants to live there.

The political-planning problem is compounded by the self-interest of political actors, whether they are in the public sector (government employees seeking more money and prestige) or in the private sector (business interests seeking favors from government). One sees a version of the calculation problem in private firms, too, especially in the case of businesses that become too large and complex for their managers to properly oversee—the executives of Lehman Brothers, for example, did not understand the problems that their firm was facing any better than did most outside observers, and less so than the most astute outside observers. But competitive markets, unlike politics, contain an evolutionary mechanism—the death of the firm. Under politics, gross misallocation of material resources can continue indefinitely—right up until the moment that the material resources run out, in fact. Democratic procedures are insufficient. As James Bovard notes, "Elections are vastly overrated as a means for restraining government abuses." Abuses are the least of it—politics paradoxically does more harm when it is performing as intended than when it is distorted by lawlessness or corruption.

More troubling, politics entangles us all in a version of the agent-principal problem articulated by the celebrated first-century economist Jesus of Nazareth, whose Parable of the Unjust Steward demonstrates that those whom we employ to look out after our interests have interests that are not identical to our own, and that in many cases developments that make us worse off make our representatives better off. That is true of corporate executives who pad their own paychecks at the expense of the shareholders for whom they work, and it is very common among elected officials and government employees, who elevate their own interests (personal, ideological, political, and financial) above those of the citizens in whose interests they are deputized to act. It isn't always something obvious and straightforward, like a regulator's offering a coveted exemption for the company at which he hopes to work after leaving government service. Simple corruption is the most obvious example of the phenomenon, but again it should be kept in mind that such venality, while troublesome, is a relatively minor part of the political problem. In the broadest terms, a politician is better off supporting an imprudent but popular policy over one that is prudent but unpopular, thus, for example, the persistence of unhealthy fiscal deficits in the United States under presidents and Congresses of both parties. Politicians have strong incentives to spend, strong incentives not to raise taxes, and (for now) the ability to use deficit financing to disconnect the pleasures of appropriation from the pains of expropriation. The defect in the political feedback loop is that because costs can be shifted onto powerless third parties (future taxpayers at present sucking their thumbs in kindergarten or yet to be conceived) it hurts less to run large deficits than it does to raise taxes or cut spending. Everybody agrees that what everybody is doing is the wrong thing, and everybody keeps doing it.

In politics there is very little reason to grow less wrong, and sometimes good reason to grow more wrong. In aggregate, this leads to destructive policy choices. This is a structural defect inherent in the political model of decision making. Substituting one political philosophy for another will not eliminate the underlying problem. The problem of politics is, for the most part, not that politics is full of bad people or stupid people; the shocking truth is that politics is full of intelligent, well-meaning people. Often they do things that they know are not the best or smartest move, and usually it is in the belief that by tolerating smaller wrongs they may serve a greater good. When this produces an outcome the public likes, that is called *compromise*; otherwise it is called *hypocrisy*, but it is difficult to tell the difference at the margins, and the shamefacedness with which politicians sometimes go about such business is probably a good sign. As the organization theorist Kenneth Boulding once observed, "Where there is hypocrisy, there is hope." But not that much hope: Politics consistently refuses to recognize the exceedingly narrow boundaries within which political organizations may maneuver effectively, and politicians instead consistently seek to extend their influence into realms in which they have no competence or the capability of acquiring competence.

Politics suffers from an insurmountable information deficit, resulting in an inability to plan. It suffers from problems associated with the self-interest of politicians and political institutions. Both of these are made much more acute by the fact that politics has for centuries successfully insulated itself from the competitive and innovative forces that produce gradual (and sometimes radical) evolutionary change in other social institutions. Each of these problems is a direct consequence of the fact that politics is, as noted, a monopoly.

But a monopoly on what?

CHAPTER 2

Politics Is Violence

Of each thing, ask: What is it, in and of itself? What is it in its own construction?

—MARCUS AURELIUS

O ri Feibush, who owns a coffee shop in Philadelphia, received a citation from the city fining him for the tons of garbage on his property, which presented an unmistakable eyesore and a clear threat to public health. Mr. Feibush agreed with the city's position entirely, save one question of fact: The property in question did not belong to him. It was all on the vacant lot next door, which belonged to the city of Philadelphia—the same people who were threatening to fine him. He had in fact spent years trying to get the city to clean up its mess. He had an idea: Since the city had finally decided that the garbage next door was a real problem, might the authorities finally be persuaded to clean it up? He made dozens of telephone calls to the relevant municipal agencies and endless trips to city buildings. He had selfish reasons for doing this, of course, namely that as the businessman next door he was suffering more from that eyesore than anybody else. He even offered to buy the land, but the city said it had other offers in mind—for a blighted property that had been vacant for nearly forty years. Strangely, those buyers never showed up or tendered offers. Finally, in exasperation, Feibush offered to clean up the lot at his own expense. The city forbade him. And then Ori Feibush did something revolutionary: He cleaned up the mess anyway, spending tens of thousands of dollars of his own money removing a shocking forty tons of garbage from the site. Once the trash was gone, he leveled the ground, planted cherry trees, and installed park benches to allow his neighbors to enjoy all he had done. Call it eminent domain in reverse.

The city responded by threatening to put him in jail, demanding not only that he cease and desist from improving the abandoned building lot but—this is the incredible part—demanding that he return the forty tons of garbage, restoring the site to its former condition.

That is politics.

I have used the word *politics* promiscuously, and possibly in a way to which you are not accustomed, without defining the term. Allow me to do so now: *Politics is violence.* Perhaps that seems too strong for you? If so, try the following experiment: Stop paying your taxes, or refuse to send your child to the local government school or a government-approved alternative, or build an addition onto the back of your home without approval from the local authorities, or have your child sell lemonade on the sidewalk without official blessing, or feed the poor in Philadelphia without government permission, and then see how long it takes for the government to dispatch to your home a team of men with guns to enforce your compliance, seize your property, or put you into a cage. The process may take a long time, or it may all happen quickly—but it will happen. In many cases, it will have many steps: citation, fine, hearing, secondary citation, secondary fine, summons, assessment of interest, warrant . . . men with guns. Treason, murder, two dollars in unpaid parking tickets, giving the homeless outlawed sandwiches for lunch—every scenario ultimately ends the same way: compliance or violence.

The necessity of large-scale cooperation is what allows nonpolitical processes—human action—to learn and evolve. Coercion is the negation of cooperation, and the power to coerce is what keeps politics from learning.

It also makes politics savage.

If you'd like an idea about the ruthlessness with which politics pursues its interests, consider the recent case of thirteen-year-old Nathan Duszynski of Michigan. Both of his parents became disabled (his mother by epilepsy, his father by multiple sclerosis) and though they received Medicare benefits and welfare support, it was insufficient to keep the family afloat. Nathan had a little bit of savings and, after reaching an agreement with the owner of a local sporting goods store, purchased a hot dog cart, with the aim of selling hot dogs in the store's parking lot. Nathan needed the money, and the store's owner believed that a hot dog stand would give people another reason to pull into the parking lot and perhaps browse his wares. The store also offered to give Nathan a commission if he commended certain products to his customers. Because the store was directly across from city hall, Nathan did the smart thing and inquired about permits, and was informed that none was needed. Win-win—until about five minutes into Nathan's first day as an entrepreneur, when city zoning authorities shut him down for unfair trade practices. The city allowed food stands, but only if they were operated by people who owned restaurants—freestanding carts, the city argued, had an unfair advantage over restaurants, because they did not have to purchase buildings or, consequently, pay real estate taxes. Michigan, home to some of the country's most dangerous urban areas, has thousands of crimes that go unsolved every year—but the case of the young hot dogger was over and done before it even began, and local authorities were clear that they acted not because of health code concerns or land use violations, but simply to protect the interests of established local businesses whose owners apparently believed that they were ill-equipped to compete against an impoverished barely-a-teenager, still years away from a learner's permit, trying to support his disabled and unemployed parents. Nathan and his family ended up homeless. Fortunately, they were not homeless in the Philadelphia suburbs, where a young woman was threatened with a six-hundred-dollar-a-day fine for feeding the homeless without a food service license.

Those who think of strong governments and active regulators as a check on the power of self-interested businessmen would do well to remember the case of Nathan Duszynski. This is hardly an isolated incident: In what has become a lovely summer tradition, children across the country have begun to operate "Alex's Lemonade" stands in memory of Alexandra Scott, a little girl diagnosed with cancer. Alex, the daughter of a well-off family, realized at a very young age that not everybody had access to the same kind of high-quality care that she enjoyed, and she starting selling lemonade to raise money for pediatric cancer patients. Alex's Lemonade stands became a national phenomenon, and men with guns were duly dispensed to shut them down—infamously in Alex's own hometown of Philadelphia—because they lacked businesses licenses, tax stamps, hand-washing stations, permits for operating food services businesses, and the like. Even those operated on private property, from the security of suburban front yards, were not safe from the dead hand of politics. New York mayor Michael Bloomberg would make a similarly inexplicable decision in 2012 after Hurricane Sandy, forbidding the distribution of food to the hungry and homeless if the salt and fat content could not be verified as being within city guidelines.

The choice these kinds of situations present us with is not the Hobbesian false dilemma of either treating little girls selling lemonade to benefit children with cancer like al-Qaeda or scrapping all of our food-and-hygiene standards, but to continue as we are or to recognize that the evidence suggests very strongly that the people we have entrusted to exercise judgment and discretion in the interpretation of our rules and standards are plainly incompetent, that the incompetence is systemic, and that they cannot be trusted. The nine-year-olds understand social welfare, and the professionals persecuting them do not. Political power cannot be reasoned with and, when the end of the leash has been reached, the philosophy is the same as that of the raptor in Ted Hughes's "Hawk Roosting," who proclaims: "My manners are tearing off heads. . . . No arguments assert my right." That is a direct consequence of the structure of politics: It is a monopoly on violence.

Here is an illuminating fact: The U.S. Department of Education owns a surprising number of guns—the *Washington Post* recently noted the department's purchase of a few dozen Remington 12-gauge shotguns with 14-inch barrels. Ownership of such short-barreled shotguns—commonly referred to as "sawed-off shotguns"—is in most cases a felony for the private citizen, but apparently the Department of Education has need of paramilitary firearms. A young man named Kenneth Wright of Stockton, California, got a good close look at them when the Department of Education sent a tactical-entry squad to his home in the early hours of June 7, 2011. They kicked down his door, raided his home, handcuffed him (he was wearing only his underwear), and then rolled him and his three preteen children into waiting police vehicles. Wright's estranged wife, who did not reside at the home, was in the department's crosshairs because of a student aid issue. (Apparently, nobody thought to knock on the door and ask: "Is Mrs. Wright at home?") Until 1980, there was no U.S. Department of Education at all, but by the turn of the century, there was a Department of Education with armed tactical squads and a paramilitary arsenal, busting down doors in predawn raids. Lest you think I am depriving you of some critical context, consider that Wright had no criminal record, much less a violent criminal record, and he was not charged with a crime. The question was purely a financial one and, it is worth repeating, did not even involve him, much less his children.

In a similar vein, in August 2012 the Social Security Administration placed an advertisement soliciting bidders to fulfill a contract for 174,000 rounds of ".357 Sig 125-grain bonded jacketed hollow-point pistol ammunition." Dozens of other federal agencies—agencies outside the national security and law enforcement departments—have similar squads with similar arsenals, used for similar purposes. Very few of them are dedicated to violent crime: On September 11, 2001, there were 2,334 federal employees working on IRS cases for every single federal employee investigating Osama bin Laden and al-Qaeda. The IRS has three times as many employees as the FBI, a much larger budget, and investigative powers that the Department of Homeland Security could only dream of. Imagine being asked to submit an annual statement to the Pentagon or CIA detailing your employment situation, living conditions, marital status, banking information, major financial transactions, net worth, travel records, etc.—the information you are required to submit to the IRS annually upon pain of imprisonment. In political organizations, allocations of personnel, funds, and other resources may be taken as a statement of approximate priorities and values. The numbers suggest that as of September 11, 2001, the federal government cared 2,334 times as much about policing taxpayers as it cared about protecting them from the terrorist attacks that occurred that day. Put another way, it was pointing a much larger number of guns at its citizens than at those who would shortly murder some three thousand of them. This is not the only possible metric to use, of course, but it is an illuminating one.

Another metric is this: In 2006, an oddball tax protester and Christian fundamentalist named Ken Hovind was sentenced to ten years in federal prison after arguing that the U.S. government did not have the legal right to tax his income. A lawyer involved in the Wesley Snipes tax protest case received a similar sentence. There is no question that these men broke the law. The interesting fact is that each received nearly twice the average prison term handed down for a homicide (5.5 years nationwide). Failure to pay taxes is routinely punished with sentences much more severe than those given for serious violent crimes such as armed robbery—which is ironic, given the extent to which taxation itself resembles armed robbery: a man with a gun demanding money.

All politics, even that of the best, most humane, most liberal and democratic regimes, ultimately rests on a presupposition of violence. George Washington observed as much in 1797 when he observed: "Government is not reason. It is not eloquence. Government is force; like fire it is a dangerous servant—and a fearful master." His views were echoed some years later by the original modern American, Henry David Thoreau, who observed: "The State never intentionally confronts a man's sense, intellectual or moral, but only his body, his senses. It is not armed with superior wit or honesty, but with superior physical strength." It is this resort to Washington's *force* and Thoreau's *superior physical strength* that I mean to indicate when I speak of *politics*. I will often use the term *politics* in instances in which you might expect to see the word *government*, because I believe (and intend to demonstrate to you) that the traditional distinction between "politics" (bad, nasty!) and "government" (civil, virtuous!) has no documentable basis in reality, and that the cop walking the beat is as much engaged in politics as the man running for president.

Politics is the art of obtaining and using the power of government. To put it another way, politics is the art of applied violence. Again, I would here ask the reader to remember that I am making an observation about the mechanics of government, not about its morality. Virtuous or villainous, George Washington or Pol Pot, violence is the fundamental political mechanism. As the German sociologist Max Weber first observed in the nineteenth century, government is *das Monopol legitimen physischen Zwanges*—"the monopoly on legitimate physical coercion." Government is the machinery of violence, and political power is the license to operate the machinery. The word *violence* of course has very negative connotations, but it is not used here in an attempt to delegitimize all political ends or violent means. It was not persuasive words that ended the Nazi occupation of Europe—it was violence. Violence has many legitimate uses. (Funny word, *legitimate*—I'll revisit that later at some length.) But even those who prefer a very broad application of political power ought to be able to recognize that vanquishing Hitler was a very different sort of enterprise from funding $3.22-per-ticket subsidies for Shakespeare in the Park performances in New York City, or offsetting overseas operating expenses for Citibank and Bechtel: Each of those federal initiatives is different from the others, but all are "legitimate" in that they proceed in accordance with the law, as enacted by a government that enjoys the consent of the people—and all are backed, ultimately, by the application of violence. If you attempt to deduct from your taxes the portion of them that goes to subsidizing Caterpillar or high-end loft apartments for artists in Memphis, Tennessee (seriously—you are paying for that), you may be sure that you ultimately will be visited by the aforementioned men with guns. In contrast, even the most ruthless multinational corporations rarely if ever resort to violence against their rivals or debtors. Goldman Sachs, to my knowledge, has never found it necessary to keep an arsenal comparable to that of the Social Security Administration or to bomb JPMorgan Chase.

Why do politicians require so many guns? Why do the Department of Education bureaucrats feel the need to arm themselves up like gangsters?

Because they are gangsters.

It may be easier to understand the underlying nature and structure of states if we briefly turn away from the case of the United States—a case in which we are emotionally invested and which is arguably unique—and consider a few examples from history. Most governments do not have their roots in the careful deliberations of an extraordinary group of Enlightenment philosophers and heroic men of action. The roots of most governments more closely resemble organized-crime syndicates, a fact that was not lost on our founders, least of all Thomas Paine, who in *Common Sense* observed of the world's great kingdoms: "If could we take off the dark covering of antiquity and trace them to their first rise, we should find the first of them nothing better than the principal ruffian of some restless gang; whose savage manners or preeminence in subtlety obtained him the title of chief among plunderers, and who by increasing in power and extending his depredations, overawed the quiet and defenseless to purchase their safety by frequent contributions." Paine was a great moralist, but again I will ask you to delay for now concentrating on the moral significance of his observation and instead to digest it as a simple historical fact, a physical and social reality with physical and social consequences.

Consider the case of Great Britain, which throughout much of its history did not have anything that would qualify as a national state in the modern sense—rather than a geographic monopoly on violence, it had competing centers of power. The king was supreme in name only; in reality, each of the barons was a force apart, each with his own administration of justice, his own police powers, and— critically—his own military forces. It was not until the time of the Tudors that anything resembling a unitary state was established in England. The early days of the English monarchy were dominated by what we moderns would refer to as "tribal warfare" if they had happened among dark-skinned people in the tropics rather than light-skinned people in the British Isles. The early stages of the monarchy consisted of an extended conflict between the Wessex kings from the south and the Danish kings from the north. It was not until Æthelstan conquered Northumbria in A.D. 927 that such a thing as *rex Anglorum*, the "king of England," seems to have existed even as a concept, and nothing like a single kingdom was established until the Danish and Wessex powers, having exhausted themselves through tribal warfare, were displaced by foreign power in the form of William the Conqueror, a descendant of Viking raiders who had established a kingdom in what is now France. The Norman power proved short-lived, and the throne of England returned to France with the rule of the Plantagenets, who were themselves thrown out in the course of an intratribal dispute that led to the War of the

Roses, with power alternating between the Lancasters and the Yorks. The last gasp of the Yorks came at the Battle of Bosworth Field, after which power was seized by the Tudor family, who crowned their son Harry as King Henry VII. Those who are so inclined can tell you a fascinatingly complex story about the putative legitimacy or illegitimacy of each of England's kings and his ascent to power, but the historical record, observed with sufficient detachment, chronicles very little more than the conflict of regional potentates, foreign invaders, and simple conquest. It wasn't dungeons and dragons; it was rape and pillage. It is only the narcotic of historical distance that allows us to regard this chronicle as a kind of romance—I am not familiar with any romantic fantasy literature set in contemporary Rwanda or Haiti under the Duvaliers, but the conditions and circumstances are roughly comparable. The rise of the English throne is a story that might have happened in contemporary Somalia, and the more one knows about it the more difficult it is to romanticize it. Even the tools of the Tudors' trade defy romance: Seen in the museum, their swords do not look very much like Excalibur but are reminiscent of the machetes associated with modern Third World conflicts. If we follow Thomas Paine's advice and burn away the mists of legend, we can only conclude that the Tudors ruled because they had the consent of the governed, and had the consent of the governed because they ruled—a consequence of possessing the larger and more ruthless army. Put another way, governments are in most cases the result of the very thing they promise to protect us against: the arbitrary use of violent means in the pursuit of narrow, self-interested ends.

As the historian Lawrence Stone demonstrates, it was the Tudors who established the first modern state in England: "The greatest triumph of the Tudors was the ultimately successful assertion of a royal monopoly of violence both public and private, an achievement which profoundly altered not only the nature of politics but also the quality of daily life. There occurred a change in English habits that can only be compared with the further step taken in the nineteenth century, when the growth of a police force finally consolidated the monopoly and made it effective in the greatest cities and the smallest villages." The Tudors set about creating that monopoly in a systematic fashion: They began by depriving the barons and other regional powers of their private military forces and, critically, of their theoretical right to maintain such forces under English law and practice. They then set about tearing down the castles and fortresses of the individual lords and weakening the traditional relationship between the lords and their vassals and tenant farmers. It is more practical to obtain the consent of the local powers when they are deprived of their military and police powers, to say nothing of their ability to collect taxes or generate revenues independently.

That lesson was not lost on England's principal rival, as the historian Charles Tilly notes:

In France, Richelieu began the great disarmament in the 1620s. With Richelieu's advice, Louis XIII systematically destroyed the castles of the great rebel lords, Protestant and Catholic, against whom his forces battled incessantly. He began to condemn dueling, the carrying of lethal weapons, and the maintenance of private armies. By the later 1620s, Richelieu was declaring the royal monopoly of force as doctrine. The doctrine took another half-century to become effective. . . . By the later eighteenth century, through most of Europe, monarchs controlled permanent, professional military forces that rivaled those of their neighbors and far exceeded any other organized armed force within their own territories. The state's monopoly of large-scale violence was turning from theory to reality.

But national military power is only one aspect of the monopoly on violence. In order for a true modern state to emerge, that monopoly must be extended to local affairs, the administration of justice, taxation, and the like, which, as Tilly reports, in due course was achieved:

> The elimination of local rivals, however, posed a serious problem. Beyond the scale of a small city-state, no monarch could govern a population with his armed force alone, nor could any monarch afford to create a professional staff large and strong enough to reach from him to the ordinary citizen. Before quite recently, no European government approached the completeness of articulation from top to bottom achieved by imperial China. Even the Roman Empire did not come close. In one way or another, every European government before the French Revolution relied on indirect rule via local magnates. The magnates collaborated with the government without becoming officials in any strong sense of the term, had some access to government-backed force, and exercised wide discretion within their own territories: junkers, justices of the peace, lords. Yet the same magnates were potential rivals, possible allies of a rebellious people.
>
> Eventually, European governments reduced their reliance on indirect rule by means of two expensive but effective strategies: (a) extending their officialdom to the local community and (b) encouraging the creation of police forces that were subordinate to the government rather than to individ-

ual patrons, distinct from war-making forces, and therefore less useful as the tools of dissident magnates. In between, however, the builders of national power all played a mixed strategy: eliminating, subjugating, dividing, conquering, cajoling, buying as the occasions presented themselves. The buying manifested itself in exemptions from taxation, creations of honorific offices, the establishment of claims on the national treasury, and a variety of other devices that made a magnate's welfare dependent on the maintenance of the existing structure of power. In the long run, it all came down to massive pacification and monopolization of the means of coercion.

Eliminating rivals, combining economic rewards with the threat of violence, buying off local officials—when thinking of the English kings, the most accurate model is not King Arthur but Don Corleone, and it is difficult to distinguish their methods from what students of organized crime would recognize as a *protection racket.* Indeed, the Sicilian Mafia imported into the United States social arrangements and practices that were not in the least illegal during the time in which they evolved—such actions were not crime, but *politics.* There is a moment in *The Godfather* that expresses the dynamic perfectly as Michael Corleone tries to justify his crime-boss father to his straight-arrow girlfriend, Kay:

> MICHAEL: My father is no different than any powerful man, any man with power, like a president or senator.
> KAY: Do you know how naïve you sound, Michael? Presidents and senators don't have men killed.
> MICHAEL: Oh? Who's being naïve, Kay?

Michael Corleone is perhaps saying more here than he knows. Of course governments have men killed—the power to use violent force is the defining feature of governments. In the exchange above, Michael Corleone was referring of course to extralegal killing, the illegitimate use of violence by government officials. That of course happens, too, though in modern democratic countries it is a rarity. But if we may for the sake of argument set aside the question of *legitimacy*—which, as the history of the House of Tudor or the contemporary government of the Russian Federation suggests, is by no means a straightforward issue—and make it a question of *mechanics* rather than a question of *morals*, we must conclude that governments operate in very much the same way that organized-crime syndicates do. We might even entertain the unthinkable thought that the Platonic ideal of an organized-crime syndicate—one that reaches its most mature and powerful expression, without rivals or constraints on its operations—would be indistinguishable from a "legitimate" government.

In entertaining that comparison, it is important to keep in mind that mafias do not rule by force alone. Historical studies have found that there exist high levels of consent and cooperation in places in which mafias are prevalent forces. Governments arose from organizations that were essentially mafias, and people living under unresponsive or ineffective governments have long turned to organizations that are either explicit mafias or indistinguishable from them, in order to obtain security. The civil war in El Salvador was indistinguishable from a mob war, and each side engaged in explicit protection-racketeering: Noncompliant Salvadorans were not only murdered but mutilated and beheaded, the purpose of which was to instill fear in the survivors and make them compliant sources of revenue, in other words, taxpayers. The Mexican cartels a generation later would do precisely the same thing.

Two recent examples, the Taliban and the Revolutionary Armed Forces of Colombia (FARC), show the character of organizations that act simultaneously as governments and as organized-crime syndicates. Like the Sicilian Mafia and the English monarchy, the Taliban has its origins in ethnic affiliation. The Pashtuns in Afghanistan and in Pakistan's Federally Administered Tribal Areas have never quite accepted the legitimacy of any government in Kabul or Islamabad—no more so than ancient Angles accepted the rule of the Danish kings of England—and those governments have never given them strong reasons to do so, barely maintaining a presence in many of the tribal areas, entirely unable to provide basic public services or enforce law and order. Afghanistan is in essence in the same condition as pre-Tudor England: a central government that rules in name only, with the bulk of the country dominated by regional warlords and local chieftains. Real governance of local affairs has long fallen on Pashtun tribal organizations, which provide security and dispense justice according to their own ancient (and horrible) traditions. A fiercely independent ethnic group, separated from a weak and distrusted central government by both culture and geography, united by tradition, language, religion, and tribal loyalties, and willing to use violence to have its way: The parallel to nineteenth-century Sicily is obvious.

Sicily was annexed by Italy in 1860 after Garibaldi and his Expedition of the Thousand succeeded in expelling the last of the Bourbons. The Italian government accelerated the process of dissolving the feudal institutions of Sicily, which had begun to break down some decades before. As a result, Sicily went from having about two thousand landowners in 1812 to more than twenty thousand in 1861, with church-owned property and other land being expropriated and redistributed. But Sicily had very little in the way of civic institutions to mediate disputes in the new era of postfeudal property rights, and the mainland Italian government had very little interest in helping Sicily to develop them, packing its courts, political bodies, and, most critical, its police agencies with northern Italians who had no cultural connections and little local knowledge of Sicilian affairs. Contracts went unenforced, fraud ran rampant, and banditry went uncontrolled.

As Oxford scholar Diego Gambetta recounts in his fascinating study *The Sicilian Mafia: The Business of Private Protection*, it was this political vacuum that created what we know as the Mafia today. The Mafia began by adjudicating disputes involving contracts and commercial transactions, and soon began providing protective services to important commercial concerns, including Sicily's lucrative citrus business. In turn, it charged taxes for its services—not unlike the 20 percent *zakat* the Afghan Taliban charges on opium crops. (In the United States, a special tax also is levied on the production of illegal drugs, though it is more of a tool of backdoor law enforcement than a stream of revenue.) In Sicily as in Afghanistan, this quickly degenerated into plain protection rackets and other kinds of extortion—though, as anybody who has dealt with police in some of the more exotic parts of the world can attest, the distinction between a crime syndicate and a law enforcement agency often can be difficult to draw with any precision.

It is important to note that what happened in Sicily, and what has happened in Afghanistan and Pakistan, was not merely the result of armed thugs imposing their will on a victimized population by brute force. What emerged in Sicily is what the Anglo-American tradition calls "the social contract," albeit an inferior expression of it. The Sicilian Mafia became, in the estimate of Italian scholar Santi Romano, an alternative legal order. As Oriana Bandiera of the

London School of Economics put it in her 2001 study, "Private States and the Enforcement of Property Rights: Theory and Evidence on the Origins of the Sicilian Mafia," landowners knowingly chose the Mafia over the Italian government as a guarantor of security. It was, in their judgment, the lesser evil:

> Historical records show that, after the abrogation of feudalism, large landowners willingly started paying the mafia to protect their properties from predatory attacks. The records suggest that landowners voluntarily passed on the monopoly over violence to the mafia, in line with the contractual view. That a conflict between the mafia and the landowners never took place provides further evidence in favour of this view. Indeed since at the time the class of large landowners retained most of its feudal power, the mafia could not have imposed its rule against their will without a fight. The fact that such a conflict never occurred and that, on the contrary, landowners often protected mafiosi from the police, then suggest[s] that the monopoly over violence was voluntarily transferred from the landowners to the mafia, rather than being usurped by the latter.

According to Taliban lore, Mullah Omar began his movement in 1994 with thirty men and sixteen rifles, after a local warlord picked the wrong rape victims (two girls in one version of the story, two boys in another). By the end of the year he controlled Kandahar Province, which has more than nine hundred thousand residents. He did not achieve that without the goodwill of the locals, any more than the Mafia came to power without the consent of Sicilians. Religious fundamentalism alone does not explain this. The

Anglo-American tradition calls it the "consent of the governed."

Understanding the Taliban as a mafia helps to give us a fuller understanding of the mechanics of politics—not only god-awful Central Asian politics, but also politics per se. Though their power has diminished, it is not uncommon today to see the very same mafiosi who profit from drugs, prostitution, gambling, and other crime acting as a kind of Sicilian version of the Saudi *mutaween*, enforcing a very traditionalist brand of public morality on adulterers, public drunks, and the like. Gambetta again:

> The mafia at times polices its territory as if it were responsible for public safety. Young thugs are recruited just to keep them off the street, and Latin lovers who harass women are not permitted an easy or indeed a long life. The presence of Mafiosi and their enforcement of moral values may be responsible for the popular impression that Sicilian women are less frequently the target of macho attentions than women in other parts of Italy.

He lists "sexual perversion," alcoholism, and crime (meaning "crime not sanctioned by the Mafia") as among the organization's concerns. Understanding the Taliban as a mafia makes it less perplexing that the same organization that enforces the strictest kind of sharia on its unfortunate subjects is also a narcotics cartel, operating in an OPEC-like fashion to intervene in the world opium markets to support prices. That is not moral hypocrisy—that is what statesmanship looks like through Pashtun eyes. Here one might note for comparison that the same U.S. government that spent $518 million to discourage tobacco use in 2010 spent $194 million subsidizing tobacco use in the same year; it has not yet taken to publicly flogging its citizens for vice, though one suspects that such neopuritans as New York mayor Michael Bloomberg must feel that temptation.

Albert Jay Nock, writing in the *American Mercury* in 1939, took note of the phenomenon and was more harsh in his judgment:

> The State's criminality is nothing new and nothing to be wondered at. It began when the first predatory group of men clustered together and formed the State, and it will continue as long as the State exists in the world, because the State is fundamentally an anti-social institution, fundamentally criminal. The idea that the State originated to serve any kind of social purpose is completely unhistorical. It originated in conquest and confiscation—that is to say, in crime. It originated for the purpose of maintaining the division of society into an owning-and-exploiting class and a propertyless dependent class—that is, for a criminal purpose.
>
> No State known to history originated in any other manner, or for any other purpose. Like all predatory or parasitic institutions, its first instinct is that of self-preservation. All its enterprises are directed first towards preserving its own life, and, second, towards increasing its own power and enlarging the scope of its own activity. For the sake of this it will, and regularly does, commit any crime which circumstances make expedient.

Given the character of the states that were most active on the world stage in the 1930s, Nock's indictment is perhaps more understandable: Joseph Stalin, a bank robber, and Adolf Hitler, a leader of riots and an accomplished extortion artist, were in fact indistinguishable from gangsters until they took on the trappings of state.

It is not difficult to imagine either of them leading an organization like the Taliban.

Or a South American revolutionary movement cum crime syndicate. In acting as a de facto local government, a crime syndicate, and an insurgent army simultaneously, the Taliban resembles another more contemporary organization, Colombia's FARC. FARC's commitment to revolutionary Marxism is in many ways similar to the Taliban's commitment to revolutionary Islam: a mishmash of genuine belief, complex loyalties, common enemies, and pure self-interest. And both FARC and the Taliban (and other mujahideen remnants) are reminders to would-be nation-builders and great-gamers everywhere that once an apparatus of organized violence has been created, it has a tendency to far outlive its putative political or ideological purpose. Deprived of its original rationale, it will discover a new one. There is not going to be a Marxist takeover of South America, but FARC will continue its narcotics trafficking operations (like the Taliban and many U.S. states, it imposes a "tax" on illegal-drug production), its ransom-kidnapping operations, and its other purely economic activities. There isn't going to be a worldwide Islamic caliphate, either, but the Taliban, like the Sicilian Mafia before it, will continue to engage in terrorism, political assassinations, and similar activities to support goals that are decreasingly political and increasingly economic, to the extent that a distinction can be made between the two.

"But that isn't us!" There are of course important differences between the British government of 2013 and the British government of 1913, 1813, 1713, 1613, 1513, etc. There are important differences between the government of the United States and the government of Haiti, between the NYPD and the Mafia. But there are also important commonalities, which are more evident if we set aside what we think government *should be* and look at what government *is*. What it *is* is structurally indistinguishable from organized crime.

True, the NYPD is not the Mafia—except when it is. Officers of the NYPD, like those of practically every big-city police department in the country (and a fair number of small-town police departments as well), have been from time to time deeply involved in organized crime. For more than twenty years, NYPD detectives worked as enforcers and assassins for the Lucchese crime family; in 2006 two detectives were convicted not only of murder and conspiracy to commit murder but also on charges related to such traditional mob activity as labor racketeering, running illegal gambling rings, extortion, narcotics trafficking, obstruction of justice, and the like. This was hardly an isolated incident; only a few years prior to the NYPD convictions more than seventy police officers associated with Los Angeles's anti-gang unit were found to have been deeply involved in gang-affiliated criminal enterprises connected to the Bloods street gang. Their crimes ranged from the familiar police transgressions of falsifying evidence, obstructing justice, and selling drugs seized in arrests to such traditional outlaw fare as bank robbery—they were cops *and* robbers. More than one hundred criminal convictions were overturned because of evidence planted or falsified by officers of the LAPD. One scholarly account of the scandal concluded that such activity is not atypical but in fact systemic—and largely immune to attempts at reform: "The current institution of law enforcement in America does appear to reproduce itself according counter-legal norms . . . [and] attempts to counteract this reproduction via the training one receives in police academies, the imposition of citizen review boards, departments of Internal Affairs, etc. do not appear to mitigate against this structural continuity between law enforcement and crime."

The Department of Homeland Security has existed for only a few years but it already has been partly transformed into an organized-crime syndicate. According to a federal report, in 2011 alone more than three hundred DHS employees and contractors were charged with crimes ranging from smuggling drugs and child pornography to selling sensitive intelligence to drug cartels. That's not a few bad apples—that's an arrest every weekday and many weekends. Given the usual low ratio of arrests to crimes committed, it is probable that DHS employees are responsible for not hundreds but thousands of crimes. And these are not minor infractions: Agents in the department's immigration division were caught selling forged immigrant documents, and DHS vehicles have been used to transport hundreds (and possibly thousands) of pounds of illegal drugs. A "standover" crew—that is, a criminal enterprise that specializes in robbing other criminals—was found to be run by a DHS agent in Arizona, who was apprehended while hijacking a truckload of cocaine. This badge-carrying mafia already is deeply integrated into politics: Its members are represented by the American Federation of Government Employees, which is responsible for millions of dollars in campaign contributions and political expenditures, about 96 percent of them to or on behalf of Democrats (Republicans have a much more adversarial relationship with government unions), including critical support to key members of the House Transportation Committee, which oversees airports and seaports, key points of interest to the agency and to the smugglers who work there.

It is important here to distinguish between differences of *scale* and differences of *kind*. U.S. law enforcement agencies engage in the same kind of criminal activities as do, for instance, Mexico's infamous *federales*, but on a different scale. Members of Congress and U.S. presidential administrations engage in the same *kind* of self-dealing and misappropriation of wealth as Russian kleptocrats, but on a very different *scale*. The differences in *scale* are the result of the presence of either healthy or unhealthy social institutions. The commonalities in *kind* are the result of the presence of political institutions per se.

The underlying theory of politics argues that the coercive powers of the state are fundamentally legitimate, though open to abuse. This belief is based in the Hobbesian notion that the only alternative to creating a monopoly on coercion is the chaotic "state of nature," the war of all against all and each for himself. Hobbes's dilemma is a philosophical construct that does not very closely represent the experience of history. People have long shown the ability to generate and enforce rules for social life in the absence of a monopolistic coercive power, from the Mayflower Compact to private corporate-arbitration services. And coercion historically has not been the only tool for enforcing contracts and policing the observation of norms: Social exclusion and informal economic sanctions have long been a powerful force in the organization of community life, for example during the pioneer days in the American West, when self-governing wagon trains operating well beyond the reach of formal government enforced their mutually agreed-upon rules by refusing to associate with those who broke them, in practice forcing violators to either make restitution or face the wilderness alone. The related concept of reputation is also powerful, as in the case of credit ratings: Individuals, businesses, and governments that refuse to abide by financial norms are either excluded from credit markets or pay punitive costs to participate in them. Prestige-seeking businesses adopt environmental standards and compensation practices in excess of what is required either by the law or the market, because there is real value in developing a reputation for being a progressive, forward-thinking business. Gas exploration firms in Pennsylvania, for example, routinely adopt environmental practices in excess of what the state's Department of Environmental Protection requires, and those firms that do not follow best practices are marginalized in professional associations. There is also some evidence that firms that adopt environmental standards in excess of the legal requirements receive more liberal treatment when there are environmental accidents or minor oversights. In an age of ubiquitous social media, the power of reputation networks is enormous—and more authentically democratic than almost anything politics has to offer. Technologically and organizationally sophisticated reputation systems are by no means a substitute for all coercive institutions, but they have the potential to outperform a great many of them.

There is a current in American political thought that regards businesses, particularly large and complex businesses, with a great deal of suspicion, and this is not without justification—businesses are collections of people, and people very often behave in destructive, antisocial, and irresponsible ways. Those who are skeptical about the ethical orientation of businesses hold up regulators such as the Food and Drug Administration and the Environmental Protection Agency as a necessary check on corporate power, but the evidence that they effectively play that role is remarkably thin. Regulators go wrong in a great many ways. Some are "captured" by the industries they are constituted to regulate, others pursue narrow political agendas, and still others are merely incompetent or ineffective. Some regulators are simply corrupt in the way police often are, and for the same reasons. Our choice is not between an ideal expression of the FDA and anarchy on aisle eleven, but between the FDA as it is and alternative means for ensuring that profit-driven actors behave in an ethical and cooperative fashion. This is by no means a simple thing, but consider the federal response to the infamous 1982 Tylenol tampering episode in Chicago: Congress passed the Anti-Tampering Act of 1983, which made it a federal offense to adulterate over-the-counter medicines—as though the state of Illinois did not already have *homicide* laws on the books to cover the poisonings of seven people. The most sensible and proactive steps were taken by the makers of Tylenol, even though they had little or no legal liability for the episode—they were worried about the reputation of their product.

There is a deeply irrational tendency in democratic societies to believe that passing a law against problem X is the same as solving problem X, when obviously it is not. There were laws against hijacking airplanes on September 11, 2001, and the box cutters used in the hijackings were regulator-approved. One cannot help but suspect that if American Airlines and United had been in charge of their own security—and financially liable for it—then they might have taken more rigorous steps to protect their $80 million aircraft and their corporate reputations, to say nothing of their passengers.

While many of us are rightly suspicious of Big Business, most Americans romanticize government. We may choose different aspects of government to romanticize—some people believe the Marines can do no wrong; others pine for the Tennessee Valley Authority—but we all tend to overestimate its abilities and its importance. Many of us regard government as a necessary evil, though few really explore the question of why and in what way it is *necessary*. (Fewer still share Henry David Thoreau's wry view that the government is "necessary" only because "people must have some complicated machinery or other, and hear its din, to satisfy that idea of government which they have.") We Americans romanticize politics in part because we are not a traditional nation-state, defined by ethnic and racial ties, linguistic and religious homogeneity, and a long history of shared blood and soil. An American may move to China, learn Chinese, spend the remainder of his life there, marry a Chinese national and raise children in the Chinese fashion, but it is impossible for that American to *become Chinese*. One does not become a Frenchman, a Mexican, or an Indian, even if one becomes a citizen of France, Mexico, or India. But one may become an American, as tens of thousands of people from around the world do every year. The American republic is unique in that it did not evolve out of a traditional hereditary monarchy, as Great Britain's parliamentary democracy did, nor was it built upon an ancient nation that has endured radical changes in the forms of government over the centuries, as the Italians, the Portuguese, and the Japanese have. The United States is practically alone among nations in that it still operates, at least in theory, under a government that was *engineered* rather than one that evolved. Of course there was evolution behind that engineering, with British liberalism having emerged through an iterated process of reforming the monarchy, establishing the Magna Carta, etc. And the constitutional order the American founders engineered was itself designed to evolve. As founding documents go, the U.S. Constitution is a splendid one (indeed, those who seriously advocate returning to governance under the Constitution as practiced in the eighteenth century are talking about something far more radical than anything I'm proposing here), and, having gotten it so resoundingly right once, Americans are particularly susceptible to the delusion that we can legislate our way out of social difficulties, and that constitutional amendments can solve our worst problems. Some cultures are based on the Ten Commandments, but ours is based on the Ten Amendments.

More so than any other people in the world, Americans look to our form of government to define us as a people. For us, the Constitution and the Declaration of Independence are very close to being sacred texts. It is true that we neglect them and routinely flout their principles, but the Bible and the Quran are no less sacred texts for all the sins and transgressions of Christians and Muslims. In the United States, we regard the government not merely as the machinery through which certain kinds of undertakings are executed but as the receptacle and expression of our highest national values, the ark of the American covenant. This attitude is ultimately destructive. We may attempt a kind of moral calculus in which we balance the Apollo space project and the Hoover Dam against Rikers Island and Abu Ghraib, but to do so is to miss the more important point that the admirable and the lamentable are the outcome of the same system, the same processes, and the same intellectual architecture. The utopian dreamer imagines that we can have our Normandy invasion without our My Lai Massacre, our NYPD heroes without our NYPD rapists, Scottsdale without Philadelphia. But it is not so. To solve the problems associated with politics, it is necessary to understand politics not only as a morally charged enterprise but also as a set of processes with outcomes that can be anticipated and that are in fact inevitable, regardless of the intellect and character of the people who serve in government office—outcomes that are, more important, inevitable *regardless of how we feel about them.*

Crime syndicates and terrorist outfits might be considered "successful" in many cases, inasmuch as they achieve their stated goals: to extort and to terrorize. Their means are consistent with their ends. But extortion and terrorism are hardly the right tools for educating children or providing medical services. Setting aside all moral questions for the moment, using coercion to achieve goals that require cooperation is simply bringing the wrong tool to the job. That is one reason why the core capabilities of politics have long been restricted to two categories of public goods—police and military—that are explicitly violent and inherently coercive. The same qualities that make the U.S. Marine Corps pretty good at its job make it wildly unsuited for other tasks. If politics has a comparative advantage, it is in killing people, caging people, and destroying property. These are things that sometimes have to be done, to be sure, but they constitute a very small part of what is important in twenty-first-century human life. The American experience in Iraq and Afghanistan suggests that the tools of coercion are not particularly good for what we now call "nation-building," though they are very good for nation-unbuilding. We are not dispatching the Green Berets to inner-city Philadelphia, but politics in Philly is backed by violence as surely as is politics in Baghdad—the only difference is that there are more steps between policy and gunplay.

But politics has become so ingrained in our assumptions about community life that it sounds radical to propose that we do not actually need men with guns to provide education or health care. It is possible to achieve much of what we rely on politics to do without entrusting an open-ended writ for the use of violence to the Philadelphia city council or to the crooks and perverts at the Transportation Security Administration. But first, it is important to understand what government is for.

What Government Is For

Politics (n.): A strife of interests masquerading as a contest of principles.

—AMBROSE BIERCE, *THE DEVIL'S DICTIONARY*

There is a lovely apocryphal story, generally told about Dwight D. Eisenhower during his time as president of Columbia University: The school was growing, necessitating an expansion of the campus, which produced a very hot dispute between two groups of planners and architects about where the sidewalks should go. One camp insisted that it was obvious—self-evident!—that the sidewalks had to be arranged thus, as any rational person could see, while the other camp argued for something very different, with the same appeals to obviously, self-evident, rational evidence. Legend has it that Eisenhower solved the problem by ordering that the sidewalks not be laid down at all for a year: The students would trample paths in the grass, and the builders would then pave over where the students were actually walking. Neither of the plans that had been advocated matched what the students actually did when left to their own devices. Embedded in that story are two radically different ways of looking at the world: Are our institutions here to tell us where to go, or are they here to help smooth the way for us as we pursue our own ends, going our own ways?

The paths in the grass were an excellent indicator of where to lay the sidewalks. Paths are a feedback loop of the sort described in chapter 2: Somebody breaks a path and leaves behind a little bit of evidence, partly clearing the way for the next person, who leaves the path even more clear for the next, etc. If another route seems obviously preferable to somebody, he takes that one instead, breaking a new path, and subsequent travelers will vote with their feet over which seems the best option. There is no Platonic ideal of the path, no right path and no rational path, only the path that seems preferable to the other paths at any given time—and paths are always changing in response to both physical conditions (rain, changes in topography or flora, etc.) and social conditions (where people are going). There may not be a *right* path, but paths have the ability to get *less wrong*. Politics is not content with paving the paths we trailblaze for ourselves—politics wants to tell us where to go. We accept this because we have mistaken beliefs about the ethical nature of politics and because we cling to false notions about the key questions of *legitimacy* and *consent*.

The concepts of *legitimacy* and *consent* are the foundation of the moralistic view of politics, which converts government from a machine for doing things into a directorate for telling us what to do. This happens on the presumption that there is some valid, underlying moral theory behind politics, based on an ethical standard to which we all implicitly consent. That is the nature of what political theorists call the "social contract." But it's a funny contract: Nobody can quite agree what is in it, and, since it was never written down, we have only arguments based on assumed principles—but nobody agrees on what those are, either. We've had a few thousand years to work out what we mean by "Thou shalt not kill," but there is consensus on that issue only in the most narrow sense. All of the issues it enfolds—self-defense, justifiable homicide, just-war theory, the morality of capital punishment—remain open and hotly contested questions. While there very well may be "right" solutions to all of those issues, it is undeniable that nobody among us—from Aristotle to Buddha to Jesus to Muhammad to Spinoza to Gandhi—has ever been able to articulate an answer to very many of those questions that commands anything like general consent, even within a single cultural group. St. Paul, in his letter to the Romans, wrote that "the law is written on our hearts"—but a lot of good it does us there! When it comes to organizing community life, relying upon that which exists only in our heads and our hearts is futile. It may seem paradoxical, but building a better world requires us to set aside much of what we have come to know as moral philosophy, at least as it is applied to politics. That is why it is important to understand Washington's insistence that politics is violence—not a seminar in morality.

We disagree about how to achieve the good life because we disagree about what constitutes the good life. Political crusaders are constantly telling themselves and their partisans that if only they could make their opponents hear reason, then their opponents would cease to be opponents and become allies. If only political candidates would say the right things in the right way, this fairy tale goes, then we could all agree on what needs to be done. A variation on this is the belief that if we could only *educate the voters* about the issues, then we could agree about what needs to be done. We have centuries' worth of practical experience in democracy proving that this is not so, but the delusion remains. People have different beliefs about values in politics for much the same reason that they have different taste in music, different feelings about family, and different beliefs about God: because we are not all alike and never will be. All political arguments based upon abstractions regarding justice, fairness, liberty, equality, and other principles are doomed to futility, because we all operate from different precepts and different first principles. If you believe that liberty is the paramount political good, then you probably will be some sort of libertarian; if you believe that socioeconomic equality is the highest political good, then you will not. But there is no way of proving that liberty or equality or some other abstraction *should* be paramount. These disputes are metaphysical, meaning that they are, by definition, beyond resolution through logic or through any process rooted in empirical evidence. Unless you are a professor paid to do so, engaging in metaphysical speculation is almost always fruitless. No valid process of reasoning can take us from the evidence of our senses to transcendent truth. Your conception of justice may be valid or it may be invalid, but there is no way to prove it in either case. We have spent ten thousand years devoted to such discussions, and we have made no progress. This distinction is less of a burden in small and homogeneous countries such as Denmark or Sweden; in large and diverse countries such as the United States or India, it is a brick wall.

Because we cannot irrefutably establish the superiority of our first principles to the satisfaction of the general public—because there is no real consensus—political entrepreneurs have been obliged to come up with arguments for forcing others to consent to their principles whether they accept them or do not. This is usually referred to in politics as establishing the *legitimacy* of a government. Legitimate governments, the arguments go, have the right to coerce citizens into following certain principles, into taking actions that they would not choose to take and forgoing actions they would choose to take. If a legitimate government decides to fight a war with which a particular citizen disagrees, then the citizen still must support the war by paying taxes or by being drafted into the army. (Thoreau went to jail for refusing to pay taxes to support the war against Mexico.) The legitimacy argument generally holds this to be the case even when the action in question is unwise, unjust, or counterproductive, so long as the government is fundamentally and broadly legitimate. Perversely, this power of government to coerce citizens into actions to which they *do not consent* is based on a criterion of legitimacy derived from the *consent* of the governed, in an ethical environment in which there is no consensus behind the consent.

Legitimacy and consent are two 180-degree arcs that together form a circular argument: A government must be held to be legitimate if people consent to it, and people must consent to it if it is legitimate. (The phrase "must consent" is, if you think about it, an oxymoron.) Using the idea of *consent* as a justification for coercing those who *do not consent* is, to say the least, an arrangement that contains a contradiction. Democratic governments hold that they enjoy a general consent that confers legitimacy upon them that supersedes the question of consent in any particular case or on the part of any particular citizen. The social contract is the only contract that somebody else can sign for you, without your consent, and still be held to be valid—and a valid expression of your *consent*, at that. This amounts to a grand philosophical sleight of hand.

Hobbes was clear-eyed about the shallowness of the stories we tell ourselves about legitimacy, consent, and the like: We accept the power of the state, he argued, knowing full well that our rulers can be immoral, capricious, and destructive, not because of some grand metaphysical principle but because of sheer physical terror. The alternative to the omnipotent state he called "Leviathan" is a state of total chaos, the war of all against all, during which life is, in his immortal phrase, "solitary, poor, nasty, brutish—and short." Hobbes's error was that he assumed that Leviathan was the only alternative to the war of all against all, rather than one possible solution among many.

But rather than embracing Hobbes's forthright approach, we still talk mostly in terms of principles. Principles are slippery at best, but *preferences* are a fact. You may not be able to demonstrate logically that we *should* elevate full democratic participation as our highest political good, or liberty as our highest political good, or economic growth as our highest good, but if you prefer one to the other, that preference is a fact. If we put a loaf of bread and a stone on a table and discover that 99 people of 100 prefer to eat the bread, that preference is a fact—and so is the preference of the one who preferred the stone. We may think of certain preferences as good (I believe that the sort of life that Mother Teresa preferred to live is admirable) or as bad (Osama bin Laden's preferences were incongruent with my own), but the fact of preference gives us a decent, concrete starting point for developing institutions that are based on something more tractable and concrete than the abstractions that have guided our politics since we gave up on the divine right of kings.

Almost all political action consists of one group of people imposing its preferences on another. While this may sound authoritarian, it is in many cases far from unreasonable: We would prefer not to be murdered, for instance, and we take steps to impose that preference on others. More precisely, we take steps to prevent murderers from imposing their murderous preferences on us. The congruence of preferences is the difference between romance and rape, between doing business and committing robbery.

The politician is the man who has the power to make his preferences mandatory.

Different people have different preferences, and, people being people, those preferences often are irreconcilable. There is precisely one kind of social arrangement by which parties with preferences that are not identical can both have their preferences met: the voluntary transaction. The genius of the voluntary transaction is that if both parties do not agree to the transaction, it does not happen. This causes us to prioritize and moderate our preferences: I would prefer to pay one dollar for a new car, and the car dealer would prefer that I pay $1 million. If I offer a dollar, the transaction fails. If he demands $1 million, the transaction fails (unless he has a particularly spectacular car to sell and a very rich buyer). I would prefer an exotic Italian sports car, for which the local Ferrari dealer prefers that I pay a price beyond my means. Perhaps we can negotiate a mutually acceptable deal, in which case a transaction happens; if not, then I go down my prioritized order of preferences until my desires and my means are congruent with the desires and means of another party, and a voluntary exchange takes place (and I get a Honda rather than a Ferrari). We all understand how that works in the marketplace. But consumers and producers, buyers and sellers, are only part of who we are as human beings, and a small part at that. Commercial processes are an integral part of modern life, an engine of innovation, prosperity, and social cooperation. But they are not all there is to life. Partisans of the free market tend to overestimate the ability of markets to help us achieve all that we want in life. For the doctrinaire libertarian, the answer to every question is either "The market will take care of it" or "Private charity will take care of it." The crudeness of these answers is part of why libertarianism remains a distinctly minority taste in American politics.

The voluntary exchange is not an ethical principle—it is only a process, another piece of social software. Open negotiation, in the marketplace or anywhere else, does not establish the priority of one set of preferences above another, nor does it morally validate the preferences that are being satisfied. It merely helps us to identify instances of overlapping preferences. That is a fairly simple thing, but it is also a miraculous one: When combined with the evolutionary social learning made possible by free innovation, it produces extraordinary results. Those include not only the remarkable advances in the material quality of life discussed earlier, but also the radical democratization of power relationships in society. As a consumer, you don't answer to the world's biggest corporation—the world's biggest corporation answers to you. And not only corporations: Entire industries and global capital structures are in the end answerable to the individual preference. As Mises put it: "The real bosses . . . are the consumers. They, by their buying and by their abstention from buying, decide who should own the capital and run the plants. They determine what should be produced and in what quantity and quality." Which is to say, consumers in aggregate perform precisely the role that Marx envisioned for his socialist central-planning agencies—but they do so without politics and without armed coercion. Unlike the politician, the consumer is not tempted to engage in political favoritism, as Mises appreciated: "They do not care a whit for past merit. As soon as something is offered to them that they like better or that is cheaper, they desert their old purveyors. . . . They bother neither about the vested interests of capitalists nor about the fate of the workers." Corporations have the power to exploit the individual—to impose their preferences—to the precise extent that politics invests its pet business interests with coercive power. You can walk away from your relationship with AT&T if you are dissatisfied with its service, but you cannot walk away from your financial relationship with Archer Daniels Midland, General Motors, or Solyndra, because they take your money through politics, the final stage of which—as previously stated—involves a man with a gun at your front door. Political projects by definition exist to mandate outcomes that are different than those that people would choose for themselves if left to their own devices. It was for this reason that the economist Murray Rothbard famously argued that political action by logical necessity never improves the overall standard of living, but merely elevates some preferences at the expense of others.

All of this renders the notion of *consent* somewhat complicated: In the voluntary exchange, we either consent to an arrangement or we do not. We enjoy what economists call the right of "exit." Under politics, we are coerced into accepting outcomes that are different from the ones that would emerge under actual consent. But the social-contract metaphor insists that we consent to being coerced into accepting that to which we would not otherwise consent. (This is one of many reasons why real contracts—written contracts—are vastly preferable to imaginary contracts.)

If government does not exist to provide an ethical foundation for society, then what is its role, if it has one? In short, the job of government is the production of what economists call "public goods"—a phrase about which there is a great deal of misunderstanding. "Public goods" does not mean "stuff that is good for the public" or "stuff the public likes" or "free stuff," though the term often is deployed to indicate one of those. Rather, "public goods" is a term with a

specific *economic* definition, and politics cannot be understood at
all without understanding the meaning of "public goods." Public
goods have two characteristics: First, they are "nonexcludable" in
their consumption, which means that there is no practical way to
keep people who have not paid for the good from consuming it. An
example would be a public sidewalk or a missile-defense system.
It would be impractical (and ugly) to try to fence off all of a city's
sidewalks and charge a dime at a turnstile for their use, and doing
so would really make a sidewalk something other than a sidewalk.
Likewise, we cannot really exclude somebody from the protection
of a missile-defense system; if I pay for a missile-defense shield but
my deadbeat neighbor does not pitch in, I still suffer if a 30-megaton
thermonuclear missile explodes over his rec room, so we need the
system to cover everybody. Nonpublic goods are excludable: If you
don't pay Apple for an iPhone, you don't get an iPhone. I can choose
to sell you a No. 2 pencil, and if you don't want to cough up the
nickel, then no No. 2 pencil for you. The second characteristic of
public goods is that they are "nonrivalrous" in consumption, meaning that if I consume one unit of the good, that does not leave one
less unit for you to consume. If I walk down the sidewalk, that does
not mean that you cannot walk down the same sidewalk. Broadcast
radio is a nonrivalrous good: If I tune in to KFMX and listen to
Led Zeppelin playing "Stairway to Heaven," that does not keep you
from turning on your radio and listening to the same station playing the same song. But a vinyl record (ask your parents) of "Stairway
to Heaven" is a rivalrous good—if I buy a copy, that's a copy not
available for you to buy. Some goods straddle the border: We have
both private and public parks, private and public roads, private and
public cultural venues, etc. Technology of course has made things a
bit tricky with some of our familiar categories; broadcast radio and

television are neither excludable nor rivalrous, but Internet radio and cable television are excludable—webcasters can charge a subscription fee. Vinyl records are excludable and rivalrous, but iTunes downloads are excludable, though not rivalrous, since an infinite number of copies can be downloaded.

The general theory of public goods holds that government must produce them because their unique qualities make their private production difficult or impossible. If everybody can benefit from a service whether they pay for it or not, then it is hard to get anybody to pay for it, in theory. But you'll notice that KFMX's broadcasting "Stairway to Heaven" fits the definition of a public good—nonexcludable, nonrivalrous—though that is not the sort of thing one would normally expect to be delivered through political processes. (NPR does not blast you with Led Zeppelin every hour on the hour, though that would improve a great deal of its programming.) The private delivery of such public goods often is funded through advertising, which is what makes it financially viable to deliver such notable and important public goods as Google through the private marketplace. It is characteristic of voluntary associations that they innovate in order to discover new ways to make projects economically feasible even in situations in which it is impossible or impractical to engage in a direct commercial interaction: Google doesn't sell you searches for a penny apiece, and Wikipedia doesn't charge you by the word for reading its articles. The two enterprises have very different models—Google is a wildly profitable technology corporation, Wikipedia is a public-spirited nonprofit—but both deliver critically important public goods. I suspect that in much of suburban and rural America, Google and Wikipedia are more important links to the wider world than the sidewalk is (though there is nothing sadder than a neighborhood without sidewalks, and the decline of the sidewalk in the American exurb is an unfortunate sign of our times).

"If PBS doesn't do it, who will?" So goes the advertising slogan of the Public Broadcasting System, which never refers to itself as "the state-run media," though that is what it is. (A wise man once remarked that the difference between liberals and conservatives is their reaction to the word *public*—when liberals hear the word *public*, they think "public television," and when conservatives hear the word *public*, they think "public toilet.") That is the fundamental argument for politics: that if we do not use the coercive institutions of the state to deliver public goods, then they will not be delivered. A corollary to that is the argument that all of the magnificent complexity of voluntary enterprise—everything from nonprofit Wikipedia articles to profitable iPhones—rests upon an essential foundation of public goods delivered by the state—which is to say, delivered by politics. "If the Pentagon doesn't do it, who will?" is a fair question. But high-order public goods—what we think of as *intrinsically* governmental functions such as the military and police—are a small part of what politics actually does. Taking the federal budget as the real measure of national-level political activity, we learn that all military and law enforcement expenditures combined amount to just under 23 percent of federal spending. (Here I've combined the budgets for the Department of Defense, the Department of Justice, the Department of Homeland Security, spending on veterans' programs, and, for the sake of simplicity, the entire Department of Energy, which has a lot of nonmilitary expenditures but also spends a lot of money on things like managing the government's nuclear arsenal. There are some law enforcement expenditures in other departments, such as Treasury, but they are minuscule, and the catch-all category of "other off-budget discretionary spending" accounts for less than

3 percent of the budget.) Much of the actual federal budget is highly counterintuitive. You'd never know it from our political discourse, but we spend more money on the Department of Education than we do on the Department of Homeland Security.

The great majority of federal spending is on nonpublic goods, specifically income transfers from one group of Americans to another, either in the form of cash payments (Social Security, Temporary Assistance for Needy Families), cash equivalents (food stamps), or, most significant, health-care benefits (Medicare, Medicaid). Social Security, Medicare, Medicaid, and combined welfare payments amount to just over 60 percent of federal spending. It should be noted that most of this "welfare" spending is not money given to poor people: People receiving Social Security and Medicare are wealthier than the average American. Business subsidies through the Department of Agriculture (which spends more money than the Department of Justice or NASA), the Commerce Department, and the Small Business Administration add up to another 3 percent of spending, much of it going to very high-income people and, in many cases, to very successful businesses. Here it is important to note that most business subsidies—what is commonly known for very good reason as "corporate welfare"—are structured as tax benefits rather than direct payments, so they do not show up on the federal spending ledger. To account in part for that fact, and for the fact that most spending (and hence most borrowing) is in the form of income transfers, I'll include here interest on the national debt (4.63 percent of spending) in the calculation, giving us about 67 percent of federal spending on items that do not come close to satisfying the definition of a "public good." (This is, I should note, a pretty conservative estimate, one that does not take into account person-to-person transfers through the Department of Education or person-to-business transfers through the Department of Transportation, or the fact that a good deal of defense and homeland security spending is really person-to-business transfers having little to do with national security interests.) Put another way, two dollars out of every three dollars the federal government spends is spent on something that does not come close to meeting the definition of a public good. If we can replace those clumsy political programs with innovative, cooperative alternatives, we will be much better placed to absorb the coming economic shock when our $100 trillion or so in unpayable bills comes due. We will also be improving people's health care, education, and retirements.

Our political theory holds that government exists to provide public goods that the private sector cannot or will not provide, but in fact the private sector does provide a great many public goods, from parks to roads, while the public sector spends almost all of its money on nonpublic goods. To put that into perspective, if the federal government limited itself to the provision of real public goods, we could abolish the personal income tax *and* balance the budget (and in fact produce a large surplus) overnight. That is not a policy prescription—doing so would be enormously disruptive—but it is a way of illustrating the discontinuity between the rhetoric of politics and the reality of politics. Almost everything in politics is taking or regulating: Telling X that he must or must not do Y, taking money from A and giving it to B. Taking comes in two forms. Sometimes we take from A and give to B because B provides a public good—B might be a soldier or a policeman, or perhaps an epidemiologist at the Centers for Disease Control. But in most cases, we take from A and give to B simply because politicians want to.

All of this gets very difficult to measure, of course, but government budgets give us in broad outline a model of *what politics ac-*

tually does. The federal budget suggests that just over 20 percent of what the national government does involves the provision of public goods, and the rest involves taking from A and giving to B because politicians want it that way. This isn't necessarily wicked or nefarious—politicians like Social Security in part because they genuinely care about the welfare of old people, and people voted for the Patient Protection and Affordable Care Act (PPACA) because they sincerely believed that it would provide relief to the uninsured and others struggling with medical expenses. Being wrong isn't the same as being evil; it's just being wrong.

The political model is constrained in what it can actually accomplish by the knowledge problem discussed above, and our theories of legitimacy and consent mainly serve to mask the substitution of violence for knowledge.

The cost of doing this is masked by the fact that the benefits of political action are very easy to see—the pleasing presence of a Social Security check—but the costs cannot be seen as readily. That is because the cost of government is *not* the annual toll in taxes and debt, but the forgone benefits that we would have derived from using all of that capital in innovative and productive ways. The $1 trillion that goes into financing the federal deficit every year is $1 trillion not available to invest in Apple (or the next Apple) or to endow the Central Park Conservancy (or the next Central Park Conservancy). The real cost of government is always opportunity cost, but that is difficult to calculate, because free societies and free people are unpredictable. The fact that we are several centuries into a very good run of making people better, richer, freer, healthier, and longer-lived suggests that we free people have some pretty good ideas about how to deploy our resources, and that wagering on our continuing to do so is the smart bet. Assets deployed in antipoverty programs that leave people poorer, in health-care programs that make people less healthy, or for national security projects that make the nation less secure cannot be used for productive purposes. We can only imagine what the world might look like if we had not spent $1 trillion on a War on Poverty that has resulted in more poverty, or roughly the same sum to drop bombs on Iraqis under the theory that eventually the ones who were left would become Swiss.

Conversely, it is also difficult to estimate the value of the public goods provided by the private sector. For example, there is a Starbucks in my neighborhood at which I have often observed something strange: The line for the restrooms is always longer than the line to order coffee—this morning, there were three people (including me) in line to order coffee, and eleven people in line for the restrooms. I counted the people in line because the previous afternoon I had overheard a woman coming out of a very expensive furniture store telling a friend (on her iPhone, of course) that she really needed to, as she put it, "potty" (grown woman in her forties, this was) but knew that there was a Starbucks nearby, and was heading there for that purpose. (It is true that, as much as I admire the iPhone, constant and instantaneous communication is something of a mixed blessing, especially for those of us in cities densely populated enough that we experience other people's conversations like we experience the weather.) Curious, I went into the store she was coming out of and, as I had expected, the establishment selling $20,000 sofas and $200 soap dishes of course had public restrooms for its customers. But in the mind of the woman leaving the furniture store, if you need a public restroom in New York, you look for a Starbucks. Unlike Paris with its *sanisettes* (heir to the justly maligned *pissoirs* of old), New York City does not have much of a publicly financed public restroom infrastructure as such. What it has is Starbucks, a privately financed public restroom infrastructure with a very successful for-profit coffee chain attached to it. Maybe you don't think of Starbucks that way, and Starbucks certainly doesn't think of Starbucks that way, but residents of New York City apparently think of Starbucks that way. In fact, when an informal mutiny among Starbucks baristas a few years back resulted in their locking up restrooms and hanging "Employees Only" signs on the doors, the public outcry was big enough that the story made both the *New York Post* and the *New York Times*. As one Starbucks manager said: "Starbucks is definitely New York's public bathroom." The city has proposed building twenty Paris-style public restrooms, but there are nearly two hundred Starbucks.

If Starbucks doesn't do it, who will?

Outside my apartment building in New York City, just around the corner from that Starbucks, there is a lovely little park. It was designed in consultation with one of the world's finest landscape architecture firms, James Corner Field Operations, which designed the city's beloved High Line park, and it boasts benches and fountains designed by the celebrated architect Frank Gehry. It is scrupulously well maintained, spotlessly clean, and, thanks to the presence of around-the-clock management, open to the public twenty-four hours a day, unlike many New York City public parks.

It shouldn't exist.

Conventional political theory holds that only the state can provide public goods such as parks, sidewalks, roads, and the like. Television commentator Rachel Maddow offered a typically exaggerated expression of this view when she visited the Hoover Dam and remarked: "When you are this close to Hoover Dam, it makes you realize how small a human is in relation to this as a human project. You can't be the *guy* who builds this. You can't be the *town* who builds this. You can't even be the *state* who builds this. You have to be the *country* that builds something like this." (Never mind that the Hoover Dam was in fact built by a consortium of private firms headed by Bechtel-Kaiser, under precisely the sort of outsourcing/ private contractor arrangement that Maddow has no time for in most other contexts—in fact, she includes a chapter in one of her books denouncing the practice.) In a sense, Maddow is correct—the Hoover Dam was an economically nonviable project from the time of its conception, and the mighty installation, visually impressive as it is, produces significantly less electricity than does a typical small nuclear power plant. Which is to say, it is a majestic boondoggle. Only politics can do that—and stay in business. And, needless to say, a "guy" attempting a project with the environmental impact of the Hoover Dam would never get permission from environmental regulators, given that its construction entailed wiping out an entire local ecosystem.

But do you have to be the government to build a public park?

The park in front of my apartment building was built by a real estate developer to enhance the value of his property, a residential high-rise. It provides a small oasis of open space and greenery amid the concrete-and-asphalt barrenness of lower Manhattan. But unlike the famous Gramercy Park a mile or so uptown, which is a fenced-in Victorian-era private park available only to residents of the surrounding neighborhood who pay a fee ("a key to the park" is a coveted renter's perk in Gramercy Square), this is a true public park, open to anybody, without charge—paid for by a private developer. The developer may have had selfish interests in mind—among other things, the presence of the park prevents the property from being put to some undesirable use and improves the view on one side of the high-rise—but the firm nonetheless produced a public good at its own expense. The only difference between my park and the one that got Ori Feibush in trouble in Philadelphia is that politics stayed out of the way. In fact, in this case, politics encouraged the private production of a public good.

Sometimes the private production of public goods is induced by regulation—New York City imposes green-space requirements on some new developments—but regulation is a minor factor in the process. You don't have to be the government to build a small park—or to run a very large one. After decades of political failure, the management of New York's Central Park was entrusted to a private trust that reversed that glorious oasis's slide into chaos, while the sprawling Appalachian Trail is maintained by volunteers. The American landscape is dotted by volunteer fire departments and private conservancies, while for-profit organizations are at the cutting edge of educational research and innovation.

The case of Central Park is especially worth considering in that it captures in miniature the econo-political dynamic characterizing our national politics. As the quality of the park began to decline (along with the general quality of living in New York City) throughout the 1960s and 1970s, its dysfunction and disrepair, vandalism, muggings, and prostitution came to be regarded as the new normal, an inevitable expression of urban realities. The city's parks department was remarkably resistant to change, and remained so until the late 1970s, when a fiscal emergency—the city was on the edge of bankruptcy—forced the acceptance of changes that political interests had long resisted. The Central Park Conservancy was established by a handful of wealthy New York philanthropists and quickly attracted a small army of volunteers. They began modestly, raising funds for repairs and doing volunteer maintenance. The arrangement was at first a largely informal one, and remained so for nearly twenty years, until Mayor Rudolph Giuliani pressed to formalize the partnership with a multiyear contract to privatize the park's management.

Nonprofit activity such as the Central Park Conservancy is in many unexpected ways similar to for-profit commercial activity. Philanthropy is a business in which the profits come in the form of prestige rather than in the conventional form of dollars. Philanthropy is in a sense a business supplying the ultimate luxury good: It's what you turn your attention to when the marginal value of making another dollar is very low (see Bill Gates, et al.). The classical model of economics and much of our political discourse draws a very bright line between for-profit and nonprofit activity, but in reality the distinction is nowhere near that clear. Philanthropists in a sense may be understood as self-interested actors because the value of reshaping the world along certain personally preferred lines is to them very high relative to the value of making more money. Ted Turner cares a great deal about open spaces and the preservation of charismatic megafauna, especially carnivores. It would be an oversimplification to say that his answer to this was simply to buy up land and put it into trusts to ensure that it remains wild, but that certainly is a part of what he has done. Turner's associates are bracingly clear about the complexity of the problems they face: "Many of our projects will be controversial, slow to succeed, and fraught with uncertainty, and some may fail. The difficulty will come not because we were ill prepared or that we did not work hard, but rather that restoration of intricate ecosystems is complex, and an imprecise process about which scientists as yet know little." Imagine if during the debate over PPACA President Obama or Nancy Pelosi had said: "Many of our reforms will be controversial, slow to succeed, and fraught with uncertainty, and some may fail. The difficulty will come not because we were ill prepared or that we did not work hard, but rather because health care is complex, and reform is an imprecise process about which the experts as yet know little." That would have been true, but it is a truth that it is nearly impossible to imagine any elected official speaking.

There is an abundance of examples of how private nonprofit associations produce remarkable public goods, but even putatively for-profit enterprises are, contrary to the cartoon version of how business works, not necessarily rapaciously focused on bottom-line issues unrelated to social concerns. People create products and companies for many reasons, one of which is profit. But there are many others as well: to satisfy intellectual and aesthetic appetites, to satisfy curiosity, to enjoy the sense of freedom associated with owning one's own enterprise. The most successful entrepreneurs do not simply see a profit-making opportunity, but instead have a theory about how to do a certain thing and a powerful interest in discovering whether they can do what it is they think they can do. It is in the nature of the process that entrepreneurs are people in the minority, often a very small minority, which has two important consequences: Innovation thrives when entrepreneurs are largely insulated from politics, and the profits that accrue to entrepreneurs are inversely proportional to the narrowness of the minority the entrepreneur represents. Gambling is a not entirely inapt metaphor. The workaday corporate manager trying out a new idea is placing a bet at maybe 2-to-1 odds, but Steve Jobs placed bets at 50-to-1 odds or 100-to-1 odds, which is why it pays a lot more to be the guy who started Microsoft or Virgin than to be the CEO of an established firm. Large profits—and, let's not overlook it, large losses in the ma-

jority of cases—are built into the architecture of the entrepreneurial process, but it would be an oversimplification to think of them
as the only engine of the process. Bill Gates Jr. was from a family
with a great deal of money, and from a purely probabilistic point of
view it would have been a safer bet for him to invest his capital in a
well-diversified stock portfolio than to start a business—or to take
it to Las Vegas, for that matter: The odds of success are better at a
blackjack table than in a start-up enterprise. Gates's bet on himself
looks brilliant only in retrospect. But his becoming a billionaire was
a side effect of his pursuing a particular minority view of the role of
technology in society—not the other way around. He did not wake
up one morning and say to himself: "I want to become the richest
man in the world—how can I make that happen?" In that, at least,
Bill Gates is not atypical.

When it comes to business, there is a lot of ignorant talk about
the law of the jungle, but there are many entrepreneurial motives
that are not entirely distinguishable from those that we would call
philanthropic. In both cases, the secret sauce is love. I suspect that
one of the reasons that Steve Jobs was never committed to philanthropy on the scale that Bill Gates has been is that Jobs saw Apple itself as his philanthropic project. He did not feel the need to dedicate
his life to charity because he believed that his contribution to making the world a better place was Apple's products and the business
itself. He did give away a great deal of money, but that was as a matter of course—it was clear that rather than "giving something back"
out of his profits, he saw his profits as evidence of how much he
had given. That impression is borne out by observations from Apple
insiders: "Our goal isn't to make money," says Sir Jonathan Ive, the
designer behind the iPhone and the iPad. "Our goal absolutely at
Apple is not to make money. This may sound a little flippant, but it's

the truth. Our goal and what gets us excited is to try and make great products. We trust that if we are successful, people will like them, and if we are operationally competent we will make revenue, but we are very clear about our goal."

A more extreme version of that same kind of thinking can be found in the case of Amazon. The online retailing giant is a ruthless competitor in the battle for market share, but its executives have for some time been pursuing a strategy of keeping profits low or negligible in order to invest in the long-term future of the firm. The shareholders have gone along with this, leading the progressive commentator Matthew Yglesias to label the company "an extremely forward-looking charitable venture" operating under the theory that forgoing immediate profits will lead to strong returns at some point in the future. Amazon is an important sales channel for many other businesses, and it is enabling its partners' profits at the expense of its own. While the company is at least in theory operating with the long-term good of its shareholders in mind, it is clear that its profit motive has been subordinated to its desire to create something new in the cooperative social-commercial space.

Apple has been wildly profitable because it has consistently made things that people like. The Central Park Conservancy is enormously prestigious—the philanthropic equivalent of enormously profitable—because, like a for-profit firm, it has successfully provided goods and services at an attractive price. Amazon grows because it looks after the interests of its customers and partners. The link between Apple and the Central Park Conservancy is not economic efficiency—Apple is sitting on a mountain of cash, and the conservancy has to go begging for mountains of cash. The link is beauty. There is famously a sense of community, even cultishness, among Apple aficionados, who merrily camp out overnight in front of Apple stores to be the first to get their hands on new products. There is something more than a simple commercial interaction going on there: The best marketing and advertising in the world does not get people to sleep on the street in front of your shop. Specifically, what is going on between Apple and its customers is a sense of communication between users and designers; the unique feature of Apple products is the little jolt of pleasure that consumers get when they sense the implied presence of a very smart and exquisitely tasteful guy on the other end of the process saying: "Hey, this is pretty cool—let's try doing it this way." There is clearly something more at work in Apple products than profit chasing. Similarly, you could make a persuasive argument that the economic value of Central Park exceeds the economic costs associated with it, and that may be true—but that isn't what Central Park is for. Understood properly, profit and prestige are measures of how much social value an organization creates—but only if by "social value" we mean "the things that society actually values," rather than "the things I think society *ought to* value." It is odd that when it comes to education and health care, we speak as though the profits earned by medical device manufacturers or for-profit educational operations are deductions from the net social good rather than a measure of how much social value those firms produce.

Social value is not the same thing as a public good, but there is a long history of private firms producing what we usually think of as public goods. Our country's first paved intercity road, the Lancaster Turnpike, was privately built by the Philadelphia and Lancaster Turnpike Road Company. Los Angeles and many other U.S. cities once enjoyed trolley-car mass-transit systems built by private real estate developers to connect urban central business districts with distant new residential developments. (New York City is practically alone in that its original subway and train lines were not the work of firms with direct ties to speculative real estate investments.) These entrepreneurs certainly were driven by profit, but they were also driven by a certain vision of what the city should look like and how life should be lived in it. They have more than a little in common with the utopian communities that sprang up in the United States during the nineteenth century and with the suburban idealism of the postwar era. Both were characterized by an optimistic if subtly puritanical vision of the good life of abundance, cleanliness, and industriousness. And both were in the end undermined by attempts to impose political planning on the complexity of human life.

As the Central Park Conservancy shows, the private production of public goods is by no means limited to profit-seeking enterprises. But the scale of voluntary social activity in the United States is seldom appreciated. Privately funded and volunteer-staffed public libraries were the norm for many years, from magnificent ones such as the New York Public Library—the main branch of which was the largest marble building in the world at the time of its opening—to modest ones throughout suburbs and small towns across the country. At the apogee of WASP society-lady culture, volunteering at the local library was practically a rite of passage, an entrée into more prestigious charitable work. (It was a perfection of mid-twentieth-century American upper-class culture that the vanity of ambitious social climbers was exceedingly well aligned with genuine civic virtue, and that conspicuous consumption had not yet displaced conspicuous civic service. The WASP establishment had its shortcomings, to be sure, but its absence is today keenly felt from the Main Line to Orange County.) To be sure, in many of these cases there was some entanglement with politics from the beginning, and in a great many more an eventual entanglement with politics, which has been especially harmful in the case of the public libraries: Somehow, as library budgets ballooned and volunteer society ladies were displaced by graduate-schooled, credentialed professionals in the faintly ridiculous field of "library science," our libraries were transformed from quiet places to read a book into psychiatric wards in which homeless men masturbate to Internet pornography. The San Francisco public libraries recently installed barriers to increase the level of privacy for this activity.

Given the disconnect between how we think about politics and what politics actually does, and given that the private sector provides a great many public goods while the public sector spends its money on practically everything but public goods, it is no surprise that politicians and those who prefer to do their business through political processes back away from discussing the facts on the ground and retreat into arguments from morality. "Never mind what works and what doesn't," the argument goes; "this is the right thing to do." It is a strange argument—what does it matter if it's the right thing if you cannot do it?—but one that fails even on its own terms.

The majority of what the federal government does can be taken over by cooperative enterprise—right now. We have very good models and practices for providing people with health care, education, and retirement incomes, which I will explore in subsequent chapters. There is no obvious necessity for anything more than what the philosopher Robert Nozick referred to as "the nightwatchman state." And we may not even need that.

CHAPTER 4

Social Insecurity

The Ass and the Fox, having entered into partnership together for their mutual protection, went out into the forest to hunt. They had not proceeded far when they met a Lion. The Fox, seeing imminent danger, approached the Lion and promised to contrive for him the capture of the Ass if the Lion would pledge his word not to harm the Fox. Then, upon assuring the Ass that he would not be injured, the Fox led him to a deep pit and arranged that he should fall into it. The Lion, seeing that the Ass was secured, immediately clutched the Fox, and attacked the Ass at his leisure.

—AESOP

Ida May Fuller was one of the most successful investors in American history, racking up a truly awesome 91,570 percent return on a single three-year investment, turning $395 into $362,100. And she didn't do it by putting her money into a hot stock or exotic derivative—in fact, she achieved those returns without taking on a risk any greater than an investment in U.S. Treasury bonds. She did so just a few years before retiring from her job as a legal secretary, helping to ensure that her golden years would be comfortable.

Fuller was the first recipient of Social Security, having paid $24.75

in Social Security taxes during her working life before going on to collect $22,888 in benefits (the equivalent of $395 and $362,100, respectively, in 2011 dollars). For members of Fuller's generation, and for retirees in the following decades, Social Security was an unbeatable deal, providing them with retirement incomes far in excess of what they would have been able to enjoy even if they had worked two or three jobs during their prime years. Social Security is sometimes criticized as being in effect a Ponzi scheme (a comparison that is to some extent unfair to Charles Ponzi, who was an old-fashioned fraud but never forced anybody into his schemes at gunpoint), and it is similar to such old-fashioned scams as the one perpetrated by Bernie Madoff in that it relies on an ever-increasing pool of new "investors" to provide outsized returns to those higher up in the pyramid. The inevitable problem is that one always runs out of new investors. The men who designed Social Security knew that the population of the United States would not continue to expand forever, and that the eventual leveling-off or decline in birth rates would invert the pyramid and render the system unsustainable. Even if the system were expanded to make everybody in the world both an "investor" in Social Security and a beneficiary of the system, it would begin to collapse sometime around 2150, when the planet's population is expected to begin declining, repeating on a global scale the demographic trends seen in the United States, Europe, and Japan.

Social Security has already begun coming unraveled. The program entered a stage of permanent deficit in 2011—meaning that taxes flowing into the system will never catch up to benefits paid out—and will be able to continue making scheduled benefits payments only for about another twenty-five years, at most, according to congressional estimates. As with the other major entitlement programs, the real question facing us is not "How do we go about paying these benefits?" but "How do we go about not paying these benefits?"

Social Security is only a relatively small part of the problem. It is something approaching a mathematical certainty that the present financial obligations of the United States and other developed countries will not be made good on at their present value. The overwhelming majority of those obligations are in the form of promised health-care and pension benefits, which already represent most government outlays, though spending on the military and on education amounts to about $1 trillion per year in each category (with the latter happening mostly at the state and local level rather than at the federal level), which strongly suggests that these, too, will be radically revised downward as mounting public debts begin to impose real-world constraints on spending. The content of the public debt and the entitlement obligations, and the way in which they are to be disposed of—the question of how we go about *not* paying our bills—will be, barring some unforeseen catastrophe or miracle, the single most important fact of economic life for the next generation. It is therefore worth taking a look at these obligations in some detail, beginning with the case of the United States.

As of 2012, the official federal debt of the United States was just over $16.5 trillion, or slightly more than the annual economic output of the U.S. economy (as measured by GDP). That debt is currently on track to grow at about $1 trillion per year. Put another way, the national debt is equal to the combined GDPs of the United States and Mexico, or the combined GDPs of the four biggest economies in the world outside of the United States: China, Japan, Germany, and France. That obligation by itself amounts to more money than exists in the United States (the broad U.S. money supply amounts to just under $10 trillion), meaning that even if we could assume that the government could get its hands on every piece of currency, all of the checking and savings deposits, all of the CDs, all of the money-market funds, eurodollar deposits, and repurchase orders— all of the stuff that is collectively known as "money"—it would still be only a little better than halfway toward paying its debt. This is of course just an exercise in thinking about the scale of things: The U.S. government need not pay its entire debt all at once—and, it bears always keeping in mind, it has the power to "create" money with a few keystrokes on a computer at the Federal Reserve, which it has been doing to an unprecedented extent for the past several years. We used to talk about "running the printing presses" to make money, but even that need no longer happen.

But it is worth meditating upon the fact that even as a purely theoretical option, simply seizing all of the money in existence in the United States would not allow the government to pay off its debt. It would have to seize property—which is, after all, pretty much what politics is all about. That property inevitably would be seized from whomever it is politically more convenient to pillage, and transferred to those whom it is most important to politicians to pay, meaning major bond investors and the financial institutions that have the power to shut politicians out of the financial markets—which is the thing politics fears most: Politics is no fun at all on a pay-as-you-go basis. The charade that is fundamental to the political game— pretending that politicians have wealth that they can give away to favored constituencies rather than wealth that they can expropriate from one group of people for the enjoyment of others—does not work especially well if politicians cannot borrow money. If bills have to be paid in the present, then it becomes more difficult to pretend that the money comes from somewhere else, some magical pot of gold called the Treasury, rather than the result of rifling through the pockets of our families, friends, and neighbors. Deficit spending is in effect a form of taxation without representation, since the unborn taxpayers to be encumbered by those obligations by definition do not have a political voice, having not yet entered this vale of tears. (If that seems cowardly to you, that is because it is, objectively, a cowardly model of operation, taking candy from a baby, as they say.)

If the national debt were the only obligation we were working to meet, the challenge would not be insurmountable. But the unhappy fact is that while that $16 trillion looks pretty bad, it only amounts to about 15 percent of the real indebtedness that politics has gotten us into. The biggest debts are carefully hidden, kept off the national balance sheet like some poisonous Lehman Brothers derivatives position gone sideways. As the economist Lawrence Kotlikoff calculated a few years back:

> The U.S. has a fiscal gap—the present value of all its future spending (including servicing its official debt) less all its future taxes of $202 trillion—almost 14 times GDP. Greece, by comparison, has a fiscal gap of about 11 times GDP. . . .
>
> The *Economist* as well as all other financial media as well as virtually all economists (academic and business) and policymakers are focusing on the official debt. . . . This is minor compared to the fiscal gap, which includes all liabilities, official and unofficial. The fiscal gap is huge compared to the official debt because Uncle Sam has spent six decades accumulating massive obligations to make social insurance payments, which it carefully kept off the books.

Needless to say, things have not improved since Professor Kotlikoff ran the numbers in 2011.

State and local governments have debt, too, of course, adding up to a few trillion dollars. That debt is now of immediate interest as a number of cities slide into bankruptcy—California leads the way with San Bernardino, Stockton, and Mammoth Lake—with others sure to follow. It is possible that Los Angeles, the second-largest city in the country and the anchor of a Southern California economy that is larger than those of most of the world's sovereign nations, will slide into insolvency. The bankrupt California cities are pressing the state for aid (meaning a bailout), and the state of California, itself a fiscal basket case, will be sorely tempted to turn to Washington for a bailout when it is forced to face facts and admit to its long-term insolvency. Chicago and other cities run the same risk. The state of Illinois is likely to follow California's trajectory, and budget analysts predict that within the next decade pension costs alone could exceed all tax revenues in more than half of the states.

Even if those state and local debts are never officially and formally federalized, they should be counted up on the national balance sheet as an indicator of our present predicament. Cities, states, and the federal government are intimately entangled in one another's financial affairs, and it is best to regard their obligations as functionally unitary.

San Bernardino and Stockton went into bankruptcy partly as a result of the economic downturn of 2008–2011. But the real estate crash, the recession, and the resulting decline in tax revenues only forced California to acknowledge reality sooner than it had intended to. Had there never been a housing meltdown or recession, California's finances still would have been unsustainable, and that is because of the second category of state obligation: pension liabilities. Federal, state, and local governments have promised their employees certain financial benefits in retirement, both in the form of cash compensation and health-care benefits. But they did not set sufficient money aside to make good on those commitments. The result is that they are collectively several trillion dollars short of being able to pay those bills. Raising taxes will not be sufficient to meet these obligations. In Ohio in 2031, pension costs will take up about 55 percent of expected tax revenues, and in some jurisdictions pension costs are expected to exceed *all* tax revenues in the coming decades. Cities and states have real limits on their ability to impose taxes, because people, businesses, and capital are highly mobile within the United States. There is a reason that so few cities impose municipal income taxes: You can get away with it in New York City, but as the dwindling population of Philadelphia attests, you cannot expect people to sit still for it everywhere. Philadelphia has lost a quarter of its population since 1950 in no small part because of a city wage tax, which sent the middle class scuttling out to the suburbs, leaving behind only those too rich or (much more commonly) too poor to worry about it. But in order to make good on those pension liabilities, cities and states will have to be doubling or tripling their taxes just to maintain a few basic services and pay their pension bills. What this presages is a large movement of people and capital away from jurisdictions with such liabilities and toward those without them.

Tax competition will result in those states with the most need for additional revenues having the least ability to secure them. The worst-off cities already have savaged current services to pay for past consumption, with many of them paying more money to retired police, firefighters, and teachers than to current police, firefighters, and teachers. In San Bernardino as elsewhere, the combination of higher expenses, reduced services, and economic instability has resulted in taxpayer flight, with high-income individuals and businesses leading the way. Unlike the case of East Germany, there is no Berlin Wall to keep Americans within the jurisdiction of unsatisfactory political operations, though the federal government has considered punitive measures against those relinquishing their citizenships for tax purposes.

And of course the federal government has a pension problem of its own—not for its workers (the federal pension system is reasonably well funded at this time and has largely been converted to a "defined contribution" system, in which there are no unfunded liabilities) but for us: Just as California promised its DMV clerks and its assistant directors of dietetics nice fat retirements, the U.S. government has made very generous promises to Americans in the form of Social Security and Medicare benefits. Like the city of San Bernardino, Washington has done basically nothing to fund those obligations. Worse than nothing, in fact—the federal government has long collected a 12.4 percent payroll tax ostensibly to "pay into" those programs, but this is a complete fraud. Social Security and Medicare are structurally indistinguishable from any other welfare program, and what one "pays into" the system in payroll taxes is almost entirely unrelated to what one takes out of the system in benefits. The impression that these are something like contribution-based pension programs is the result of several generations' worth of abject dishonesty about the nature of the entitlement programs.

The result is that it probably already is too late to save Social Security in its current form, that is, that of a putatively self-financing, pay-as-you-go pension system with revenues and outlays that are, if only for accounting purposes, independent of general government finances. As Social Security trustee Charles Blahous reads the situation, there is no viable political avenue for preserving the system:

Advocates on the left sometimes argue to increase the amount of Social Security wages subject to the payroll tax. The most extreme version of this proposal would be to raise the amount of wages subject to the full 12.4 percent payroll tax—$110,100 today—up to infinity. Yet even this drastic measure would now fail to keep Social Security in long-term balance as well.

We are thus approaching the point where each side would have difficulty balancing Social Security finances even if it could dictate the solution—and rapidly passing the point where a compromise solution remains reasonably likely.

. . . If a financing solution cannot be reached, then Social Security's self-financing construct would need to be abandoned.

. . . Upon merging into the general fund, Social Security benefits would be far less secure going forward. Benefit payments would have to compete with other annual spending priorities, and would be limited to those deemed affordable given pressures elsewhere in the budget. They would thus be much more susceptible to sudden reductions, means-tests, and other episodic changes to which general fund financed programs have long been subjected.

If this all happens, and renders tomorrow's Social Security benefits less secure than today's, it would be a tragic irony: the outcome would have been brought about largely by supporters of Social Security having countenanced the tactics of delay to the point that the program's unique political protections could no longer be preserved.

All told, we're talking about mind-bogglingly large liabilities: At present, the total bill adds up to something on the order of $130 trillion to $150 trillion by my estimate, more than $200 trillion by Professor Kotlikoff's count—for the United States alone. That is not only more than all of the money in the United States, it is more than all the money in the world—about twice that, in fact. It is about twice global GDP, and more than the value of all the assets in the world—from household items to real estate and stock portfolios—combined. Other advanced countries have similar debts and liabilities on a smaller scale, and all will be competing in the global capital markets to borrow money to finance them. There are many possible outcomes here, but there is no plausible scenario in which all of these obligations are made good on. To maintain the main entitlements alone (to say nothing of the pensions, national debt, and future spending) would require the U.S. government to roughly double all federal tax rates. We could raise the income tax on those earning in excess of $250,000 a year to 100 percent and still find ourselves far short of being able to pay those bills. It simply is not going to happen: Reality is not optional.

Most of these economic analyses neglect an important variable: interest-rate risk. The cost of financing federal debt is currently near historic lows, in part because of the capital flight associated with the European economic crisis. If the cost of financing the federal debt should return to its historic average, that would blow a Pentagon-budget-sized hole in government finances. If debt-financing costs should return to their mid-1970s levels—hardly an impossible scenario—then interest on the debt would be the single largest item in the federal budget by a long ways, equal to about *twice* all current discretionary spending. Interest on the debt is the one item in the federal budget for which spending cannot be reduced, unless the government defaults on its debts, which would produce a global economic catastrophe of proportions unprecedented in modern history, the outcome of which would be entirely unpredictable. Washington, then, will be faced with a choice of which howling mob it wants to face: recipients of Social Security and Medicare benefits or the world bond market. One of these groups has the power to cut the federal government off from global credit markets, and one does not: Don't bet on grandma.

It should be noted that the recent deficit and spending profiles under putatively conservative governments—President George W. Bush and a unified Republican Congress—have not been very good: between $500 billion and $600 billion a year. Recent deficits under putatively liberal ones—President Barack Obama and a unified Democratic Congress—have typically run between three and four times that amount: between $1.6 trillion and $1.9 trillion. Deficits under recent mixed governments also have run quite high: about $1 trillion with President Bush and a Democratic Congress, about $1.2 trillion with President Obama, a Democratic Senate, and a Republican House. And while a great deal of attention is paid to marginal discretionary-spending concerns (foreign aid, the National Endowment for the Arts, Big Bird) and to relatively small amounts of military spending (the wars in Iraq and Afghanistan did not constitute a particularly large part of the national defense budget), the congressional caucuses of both parties are relatively mum on the entitlements, which are the major drivers of future deficits and liabilities. When President Bush proposed a fairly ambitious program to reform Social Security, Republicans and a great many movement conservatives walked away from him, and the question of entitlement reform remained more or less dead until taken up by Representative Paul Ryan, whose incrementalist reform program stalled in a split Congress and did very little to advance the ambitions of the Romney-Ryan presidential ticket in 2012.

State and local governments probably will default on some of their pension obligations, if only because the alternative is closing their schools and police departments. But there are complications: In many jurisdictions, there is either statutory law or a constitutional provision making it illegal to reduce or default on those pensions, and that will end up being an interesting legal case study. The law says that governments have to pay their pensions, but governments do not have the money and cannot raise it through borrowing (the markets already are cutting them out, in California and elsewhere, as this is written) and they cannot raise it through higher taxes, either. Just as there are laws directing that pensions have to be paid, there are laws limiting tax rates as well. More important, there are economic realities limiting tax rates, too: If San Bernardino were to impose a 50 percent local income tax in order to meet its obligations, most everybody with the means to do so would simply move a few miles down the road to Rancho Cucamonga, leaving San Bernardino with fewer local taxpayers and a collapsing local property tax base as well. This is an extreme example, but more modest measures create proportional economic pressures, and indeed San Bernardino already is experiencing the flight of its wealthier and higher-income residents, and businesses are reluctant to locate facilities there. California at large is experiencing similar problems. Silicon Valley icons such as Apple are not ready to pack up and leave, but they are expanding operations in places such as Austin (Texas has no state income tax and relatively stable public finances) rather than in California.

What is true of San Bernardino and of California also is true of the United States. Because the United States has the highest corporate income tax rate in the developed world (having recently out-paced Japan on that front), and because the United States practically alone in the world maintains an extraterritorial tax law (meaning that profits earned abroad are in most cases taxed a second time in the United States once the money comes home, rather than once at the local rate where the profit was earned), there are several trillion dollars in earned profits that U.S. firms will do everything they can to avoid bringing back to the United States and its punitive business taxes. Wealthy individuals do the same thing. The past years have seen record numbers of Americans relinquishing their U.S. citizen-ship in order to live under friendlier tax regimes in places such as Switzerland, and the wealthiest Americans form small corporations in foreign jurisdictions in order to protect their money from high levels of taxation. The economic reality is that you can raise taxes only so much. The middle class and the poor have limited funds, and the rich and international businesses have unlimited options. And access to increasingly sophisticated financial services means that the middle class increasingly has access to tax-avoidance strate-gies once reserved to the rich.

Because a small handful of programs—Social Security, Medi-care, Medicaid, and related welfare programs; national security; and interest on the debt—constitute about four-fifths of federal spending, a radical reconfiguring of the entitlement/welfare state would amount to a radical reconfiguring of the federal government itself. The U.S. government is, in an important sense, a promise—a promise that is not going to be kept. The national security appara-tus, which is second only to Social Security as a federal expense, probably will undergo deep revision, partly for economic reasons and partly for noneconomic ones, but for the moment I'd like to concentrate on the case of the entitlements.

There are basically three ways in which the federal government can go about not paying its obligations. One is by explicitly defaulting on creditors, with catastrophic consequences. The second is "monetizing" the debt and entitlement liabilities, which means artificially creating money, debasing the coin of the realm and nominally paying those benefits in increasingly worthless dollars. This, too, would be enormously socially disruptive. The third is implicitly defaulting on taxpayers, eliminating the entitlement programs as we know them, which would probably mean, at the very least, limiting payments to the very poor. This, too, would prove socially disruptive and have serious economic consequences. American households are planning on receiving trillions of dollars in Social Security, Medicare, and other federal benefits, which are going to disappear in much the same way housing equity did when the millennial bubble collapsed. Indeed, it is not too much to regard the current run-up in unfunded Social Security and Medicare liabilities as an "entitlement bubble" analogous to the housing bubble. It is impossible to predict with any precision what the outcome of this will be, but a long and deep recession—perhaps lasting decades—is a real possibility.

The economically inclined will see in the entitlement state something very much like a "tragedy of the commons." The size and scope of the entitlement programs is so vast compared to the collateral underlying it—in other words, all of our wealth—that all private property has in effect been rendered common. The entitlement programs, however well-intentioned, are an invitation for everybody to pillage everybody else as a retirement planning strategy. The economist Hans-Hermann Hoppe recognized that as the fundamental flaw of the modern, democratic welfare state: "A 'tragedy of the commons' was created. Everyone, not just the king, was now entitled to try to grab everyone else's private property. The consequences were more government exploitation (taxation); the deterioration of law to the point where the idea of a body of universal and immutable principles of justice disappeared and was replaced by the idea of law as legislation (made, rather than found and eternally 'given' law); and an increase in the social rate of time preference (increased present-orientation)." The eighteenth-century French economist Frédéric Bastiat referred to government as "the great fiction by which everybody attempts to live at the expense of everybody else." The result in the United States is a combination of debt and unfunded liabilities that far outstrips all of the wealth on this planet.

The crater that will be left after the fiscal bomb goes off will be very large indeed. What shall we put in it?

How about real wealth? Obviously, if everybody were as wealthy as Bill Gates, we would not need Social Security or Medicare. So why not just give everybody a check for $50 billion? The idea is of course absurd. All of those dollars are just little colored pieces of paper or lines of code in a bank computer. But then again, those trillions in promised government benefits are no more substantial. So why not just write checks? The usual answer one will hear most often is "inflation," but rising prices would only be a symptom of the underlying condition: scarcity. Writing gazillion-dollar checks to every American would not leave anybody better off, because doing so would do nothing at all to increase the production of real goods—and real goods, not money, is what makes a society wealthy. Money is just a way of keeping count and facilitating exchange. Unfunded entitlement promises are exactly the same thing as writing the American public a $100 trillion check and printing the dollars to pay for it. Being a creature of politics, the entitlement system is focused entirely on the *consumption* of goods, not on their *production*. Politics, as usual, is looking through the wrong end of the telescope.

What happens when you subsidize consumption rather than production? Understanding that is key to understanding the entitlement problem. For the purposes of illustration, consider a much simpler real-world case from my own recent experience: renting parking spaces at the commuter train station in Stamford, Connecticut. The train station is government-owned and therefore politically operated, and the price of parking spaces is a real bargain: about seventy dollars a month, which is much less than spaces in nearby apartment buildings and parking garages, and considerably less than the $600 a month that Manhattan-bound commuters would expect to pay near their Wall Street or Midtown offices. (Similarly, Social Security benefits have been a real bargain for retirees for many decades, with benefits paid far exceeding taxes paid for relatively long-lived populations, such as middle-class white women like Ida May Fuller.) The problem with that superb deal on renting a parking space is that you can't rent a parking space. There are thousands of people on a waiting list for those spaces, and it typically takes years of waiting to get one. Stamford and nearby Greenwich are bedroom communities full of young New York financial and media workers, a great many of whom come and go between positions and locations every few years. As a consequence of that, the people who are actually able to rent parking spaces disproportionately are not the relatively young commuters who take the train into the city every day but older, long-established local Connecticut households populated disproportionately by noncommuters. You would be right to guess that this has led to a thriving black market in parking permits in some Connecticut commuter towns. But notice what has happened here: The transit authorities offered parking at a below-market price, meaning that they offered a subsidy to *consumers* of transit services. But that subsidy created no new parking spaces, and so it has resulted in a *lower* level of consumption by actual commuters and created incentives for local noncommuters to consume parking spaces that they would not ordinarily consume. It's a great deal that leaves its intended beneficiaries worse off. The economics of the question are hotly contested, but it is very likely that the diversion of large amounts of money into the health-care sector (through entitlements and the preferential tax treatment of employer-based health-care benefits) has replicated that effect on a grand scale. The pool of money chasing available goods and services is growing more quickly than the pool of goods and services, resulting in the massive inflation of health-care costs that have characterized the industry for several decades.

Sometimes, subsidies lead to higher levels of production. U.S. agricultural policies subsidizing the production of corn and wheat have, to nobody's great surprise, led to the production of vastly more corn and wheat than otherwise would have been produced, to the extent that producers have had to engage in a great deal of political innovation to secure consumers for that extra grain in order to prevent a price collapse. The corn farmers hit upon the same solution that the insurance companies employed when faced with the PPACA: Have the government pass a law forcing consumers to buy their product. Economists, including those within the energy industry, are practically unanimous in their belief that without the federal mandate that corn-derived ethanol be added to all gasoline, neither the product nor the additional corn crops that support it would be economically viable. Ethanol as a product would practically cease to exist without the mandate that it be consumed. Mandates aren't the only way to suck up excess production, of course. There are many agricultural economists who believe that the prevalence of high-fructose corn syrup as an ingredient in processed foods is largely a result of subsidies that make it more attractive than conventional sugar, which itself is kept artificially expensive by excluding imports from the market. It is remarkable that at the same time we are issuing record amounts of food stamps we are taxing the poor to pay for government programs that are designed to make their groceries more expensive. It is a head-clutchingly asinine thing to do, but then politics attracts asses of exceptional asininity.

It is relatively easy to change agricultural output in response to political incentives. If the government starts writing big checks for cotton, wheat, corn, and soybeans, then it probably makes sense to switch some share of one's cropland to those crops and away from nonsubsidized crops. But not all production is so malleable. A field can be switched from one crop to another in a matter of months or weeks, but it takes a long time to build a hospital, to train doctors, nurses, and other medical professionals, or to build a factory in which to construct MRI machines. Health care isn't soybeans.

As with the Connecticut parking spaces, we have through the entitlements (and through the tax preferences given to employer-based medical benefits) done a great deal to encourage the consumption of health-care services while doing nothing to encourage the production of them. In fact, various political efforts at health-care reform going back decades have made it less profitable, less prestigious, and less enjoyable to be a doctor, with the result that our best and brightest no longer even consider medicine to the extent that they once did, preferring jobs in finance. About one in four U.S. doctors today is an immigrant, meaning that without high levels of immigration the number of medical professionals would be nosediving relative to the population. Life as an American doctor looks pretty good to a recent med school graduate in Bombay or Karachi, but not to a

Harvard-bound valedictorian at an American high school. But even with immigration, the number of physicians in many specialties has stagnated, and new policies in the PPACA, such as punitive taxes on manufacturers of medical devices, will contribute toward stagnation in other sectors of the health-care industry if they are enacted. And while there is some concern nationally about the number of doctors in the general profession, there is acute concern about the number of doctors who are willing to see patients enrolled in Medicare, Medicaid, and other government-run programs. Medicare ends up being a great deal on insurance to pay doctors who will refuse to see you. Medicaid is of course even worse: The quality of the doctors and institutions that will take Medicaid patients is so low that they have worse health outcomes than do those with no insurance or coverage at all. Subsidizing consumption of a good does not necessarily ensure that production will keep up with demand; it merely replaces the most efficient and fair form of rationing (market pricing) with inefficient and politically biased forms of rationing. Even before the passage of the PPACA, about half of all health-care spending in the United States was government money. (For that reason, if for none other, the conservatives' cries of "socialized medicine" during the PPACA debate were odd.) New Deal policies that tied workers to employer-based insurance programs, and later policies such as the creation of the HMO, simply resulted in the rationing duty being handed off to insurance companies, as they no doubt will continue to be under the PPACA, should the program survive.

You can give retirees X dollars in health-care benefits, but that is not the same as giving them health care. Even if Medicare were not on the verge of collapsing under its trillions of dollars in unfunded liabilities, it is not clear that sustaining it would do much to increase older Americans' access to the health-care services they actually need. As noted, about half of all U.S. health-care spending before 2010 was government money, and the economist Robin Hanson estimates that about half of all U.S. health-care spending produces no meaningful benefit in terms of medical outcomes. One suspects that there is a great deal of overlap between the categories of "government-funded" and "producing no benefit," if only because together they add up to 100 percent of U.S. health-care spending. One possible way to ameliorate that is to divert resources from subsidies for private health-care consumption to something more closely resembling a public good, as economist Tyler Cowen of George Mason University argues: "Always convert dollars of benefits, usually a private good, into dollars of support for medical research and development, a public good. You will never end up at a margin where this is a bad trade."

Social Security was an extraordinarily good deal for the first beneficiaries. Over time, the program has become less and less of a good deal, and will continue to do so. And it looks even less attractive relative to plausible alternatives. In 2012, the average Social Security benefit ran just over $1,200 a month. For that, you're taxed 12.4 percent of your take-home pay from your first day of work until your last. All but a small group of high-income workers pay that tax on nearly 100 percent of their income. Compare that to this: A married couple, each earning ten dollars an hour and investing only 10 percent of their earnings at a modest 5 percent return, retires with an annual income of about $50,000 a year—assuming they never touch the nearly $1 million principal they'll leave to their children. (That 5 percent is conservative: The average inflation-adjusted return on the S&P 500 since 1950 has been 8.62 percent. Assuming an 8 percent return gives the theoretical couple above nearly $3 million for retirement.) That $50,000 a year represents about three and a half times the average Social Security benefit—and, unlike Social Security, it is not subject to downward revision should politicians decide doing so is desirable. President George W. Bush was mocked for calling his proposal to cultivate such minimum-wage million-aires the "Ownership Society," but it was the most important ini-tiative of his presidency, one that would have entirely remade the American economy. A pension system in which workers spend fifty years investing in the real marketplace and earning real returns will radically transform everything from retirement planning to corpo-rate governance—and will shift trillions of dollars in capital away from politics and into investments in real goods. Most important, such pensions would be heritable—enabling the building of multi-generational wealth in communities in which that currently does not exist. Solving the problem of poverty among the young begins with solving the problem of pensions for the old. We can do that for less than most Americans are paying in Social Security taxes today.

There are some tall obstacles to the happy scenario above. The first is that it is essential that people begin saving a substantial amount of money for retirement very early—preferably in the first year of their working lives. In fact, they should begin planning for retirement even before that. It would be enormously beneficial if families or some other institution began seeding retirement funds for individuals at the time of their birth. A dollar with an extra twenty years of compounding growth is far more valuable than ten dollars put in during the years immediately before retirement. (Fifty bucks a week starting from birth produces a retirement nest egg of $1.6 million at 5 percent returns, or $5 million at 7 percent returns.) Short of passing a law establishing a more generous version of the individual retirement account and using the government to force people to divert 10 percent of all earnings into them until retirement, how might we overcome that problem?

The simplest method is to begin with an opt-out provision for Social Security. People who understand the benefits of deferring consumption in order to invest for retirement should have the option to act on that knowledge using their own resources. Laws should be reformed allowing parents to invest on behalf of their children, and the tax code should be reformed in such a way that retirement savings can be taken out of pretax income with no taxes on the proceeds and no taxes on inheritors of such accounts. If we want people to make responsible decisions, we should begin by ceasing to punish them for making responsible decisions. On the individual level as on the macroeconomic level, much useful social innovation happens through imitation: When people see the benefits of life-long investing, they will want to realize the same advantages for themselves and their families. Critics will point out that this opt-out would contribute to the deteriorating financial condition of the traditional Social Security system. My own inclination is to regard that as a benefit rather than a cost: The sooner we start moving capital away from politics and into productive enterprises, the better.

Middle-income and high-income people can be largely relied upon to save and invest for their retirements—they already do so in large numbers. But what about the poor? They have less money to invest. They are less financially sophisticated and (forgive me for being so patronizing as to notice the vast reams of data on the subject) less inclined in general toward making responsible personal decisions. Without a coercive system in place to force them into a politically mandated retirement savings program, how can we expect anything other than for them to end up on the street destitute?

What we need is a social contract—a real one, not an implicit one. Politics is based on involuntary wealth transfers, which are conducted through programs that are, almost by definition, wasteful and inefficient, oriented toward immediate consumption rather than toward the long-term accumulation of real assets, and characterized by the economic dysfunction inherent in all politically managed systems. The easiest immediate solution to the problem of involuntary wealth-transfer programs is voluntary wealth-transfer programs.

We are very, very wealthy people, we twenty-first-century advanced-economy workers, and for those of us at the higher levels of income and wealth the price of engaging in charity is likely to be very low—we aren't going to miss any vacations or eat worse food because we offer up some sum of money to help the poor or others in need. The costs for us are very low, and the benefits for the recipients are very high. And to take a selfish point of view, engaging in a modest level of voluntary wealth exchange could leave us better off, too, if we do so under a program (or a group of programs) that is future-oriented, meaning that it is designed for the purpose of capital accumulation rather than to subsidize immediate consumption.

One of the consequences of understanding the limitations on human beings' power to plan and predict the future is that those of us who are critical of political planning rarely have a satisfying answer when the inevitable question arises: "Okay, what's your plan?" We do not have a single plan or imagine ourselves endowed with godlike powers to predict the future needs and wants of hundreds of millions of people under economic and political conditions that are utterly unknown. With that caveat, consider something I call "the Mortgage," an illustrative example of the sort of thing that we could cooperatively achieve to replace politics with something that works. While the Mortgage is not something that I expect to see happen (and not even something I would necessarily want to see happen), it is a good stand-in for what a voluntary wealth-transfer program might look like in aggregate.

The Mortgage is based on an important fact: Our ability to improve the lives of the poor—not only the so-called deserving poor, who are unable to care for themselves, but also people who simply have made bad decisions or suffered a long streak of bad luck—is not too terribly constrained by a lack of wealth. We are fabulously wealthy. And some of us more so than others. U.S. taxpayers (individuals, couples, and businesses) with incomes in excess of $100,000 a year collectively make about $4.5 trillion in a typical year (2008 is the last year for which IRS figures are available). That sounds like a lot of money—it *is* a lot of money—but it is not that much in the context of a country as populous as the United States. If we wanted, for example, to provide fairly generous benefits equivalent to $10,000 a year individually (or $40,000 for a family of four) for every American living at 125 percent of the poverty level or below (there were a record 66 million of them in 2012), that would cost those high-earning Americans about 15 percent of their total income, which is very nearly what they paid in federal income taxes in 2008 (about 18 percent), and those taxes had to support much more than programs for the poor. And while an extra ten grand per impoverished individual would make a real difference, it is not going to be a socioeconomic game-changer. And members of the $100,000-and-up set are not necessarily all that rich, certainly not millionaires across the board: A great many of them are married couples in which each partner is earning $40,000–$75,000 a year. There were in 2008 about 14 million tax returns for households earning $100,000 to $200,000 a year, but only 3.4 million earning $200,000 to $500,000, and the numbers fall off sharply from there. Only 13,000 households earned

$10 million or more, meaning that subsidizing the day-to-day consumption of the poor out of their incomes would be relatively burdensome. More important: The way to make the poor wealthy is not to give them income—the way to make the poor wealthy is to give them wealth.

Instead of writing monthly checks to the poor, a far better approach would be to begin right now—before the coming fiscal crunch—voluntarily investing on their behalf, accumulating capital rather than enabling immediate consumption. Like a mortgage, this would be a thirty-year financial plan to secure a real asset, in this case a trust fund for the poor that, unlike the Social Security and Medicare trust funds, would have something of real value in it. If Americans earning $100,000 or more invested a mere 5 percent of their incomes for thirty years at a 6 percent return, this one-time investment would provide a trust fund of more than $20 trillion. (Six percent returns look admittedly optimistic in 2013, but that is below the historical average return on equity investments.) A more conservative forty-year investment at 5 percent gets you $30 trillion, a fifty-year program some $53 trillion. A $20 trillion trust fund could reasonably expect to generate $1 trillion a year in income, enough to seed retirement trusts for every child under seventeen years of age in the United States (and there will be 100 million of them by 2050) to the tune of $5,000 a year—forever—while reinvesting half of the profits. A one-time, long-term investment could ensure that every child born in the United States could look forward to an extra $2 million to $3 million at retirement, or used judiciously for key investments in things like education and health insurance over the course of their lifetimes. (And if we limited these subsidies to the nonwealthy, we could of course be even more generous.) There are many ways a single generation can change the world. Having the well-off kick in 5 percent for thirty years isn't the Normandy invasion, but it would be quite something nonetheless. My own sense is that the great majority of high-income Americans would not resent investing 5 percent on behalf of the less well-off. Indeed, there are a small number of well-off Americans today clamoring for higher taxes on themselves, though that is a distinctly minority position—not because the rest of the rich are remarkably selfish, but because they instinctively know that money given to politics gets used for politics, for all of Washington's hollow talk about "investment." If we'd started making a real investment for the poor in 1965 instead of enacting Medicare, we'd already be there.

The Mortgage need not represent a single plan. In fact, it almost certainly would be better if it did not. It is more of a mental model for what kind of cooperative action is possible. What is needed is hundreds of projects along those lines—an education trust, a retirement trust, a health care trust, an unemployment trust. It is one thing for market-oriented reformers to argue for lower taxes and lighter regulation; as desirable as those things may be, real social change will come from taking direct, voluntary action to do in reality what politics proposes to do in theory but never actually achieves.

Why invest for the poor? For the well-off, paying 5 percent into a productive program is better than paying 50 percent (or more) into unproductive ones, which is the direction we're headed right now. The rich may take an even more narrowly self-interested point of view, of course: If we do not help the poor, they may be more likely to commit crimes or cause other kinds of social disorder, and they may be more interested in using politics to pillage their wealthier fellows if they do not receive some kind of assistance. There probably is something to that line of thinking, though a good deal less than many aggressive egalitarians believe. Still, it is an impoverished point of view. Are our fellow citizens nothing to us other than de facto blackmailers, who must be paid off to avoid violence or wanton expropriation? We would do better to regard human beings as assets than as liabilities—potentially productive and creative entities, not mere mouths to feed. I would hope that those who share my preference for cooperative human action would not take the narrow point of view. The freedom to engage in cooperative action is not an abstract good. It is good because it is good for people.

Human beings engage in acts of charity—meaning simply the act of taking care of other human beings—because we believe that human beings are valuable. Even those of us who believe very strongly that people should be expected to care for themselves and to be responsible for themselves—who believe that this responsibility is a big part of what it means to be human—must surely understand that there are those who cannot do so: young children, for example, or those with severe mental and physical disabilities. We tend to want to take care of those people first because we believe that they have no culpability for their condition, as indeed they probably do not. And while I will not ask you to accept any moral maxims from me, I will say that I believe that an even better sort of charitable impulse includes helping those who are to some degree culpable in their condition. There are drunks and addicts who became drunks and addicts because of their own actions, and there are people who are in effect excluded from participating in the economy because they committed crimes, and people who are in bad conditions because they made bad decisions, and maybe continue to make them. But those who value human life might value human lives even in cases in which the owner of that life does not seem to value it very much. While the question of culpability probably should not be ignored or discarded, or even minimized, it need not always be the controlling criterion for those inclined toward helping people. That is one reason for investing on behalf of the poor.

Another is the possibility of maximizing the use of human capital. We have a long tradition of establishing scholarships for the poor, because we recognize that inevitably in any poor community there will be talented and enterprising people who are unable to make the most of their lives because they are lacking crucial access to education and other opportunities, especially in their early lives. Sensible societies scour the kindergartens and the elementary schools to identify the best and the brightest, and those with rare talents who may not be able to flourish without some assistance. This is a rationale for investing for the poor that is partially self-interested, but not entirely so: We want to make a better world, and it is a happy consequence that, if we are successful, we get to live in it.

CHAPTER 5

Health Care Is a Pencil

The Buddha's teachings were founded on the awareness of the three impediments of old age, sickness, and death. The Enlightened One, if he had meditated on it, would not necessarily have rejected a technical solution.

—MICHEL HOUELLEBECQ, *THE ELEMENTARY PARTICLES*

The price of health care is high because there is no price for health care.

Some years ago, I found myself needing a medical procedure at the same time I was considering changing jobs. It was a possibility that I might find myself without health insurance and paying for the procedure out of pocket. In order to calculate how I should modify my plans, I began calling around to various medical practices and inquiring as to the price of the procedure. It was nearly impossible to get an answer other than "Let's see if your insurance covers it." I was quite insistent that I needed a price that I could rely upon in the event that I needed to pay out of pocket, a proposition that seemed to universally mystify every medical professional with whom I came in contact. After dozens of phone calls to several medical practices—including some very prestigious ones—the answer was the same:

"Talk to the lady in insurance." When I finally succeeded in getting an estimate from one doctor, the possible price ranged from the low five figures to the low six figures, the higher end of the estimate being more than ten times the lower end. Strange that I can get an exact price on an iPhone, a Honda Civic, or a pizza, but not on something as essential to my well-being as health care.

There are almost no consumer prices in health care. Because there are no prices, there is no price discrimination by consumers, and therefore no pressure to keep prices down to where consumers can pay them. It's a chicken-and-egg problem: One of the reasons that we rely on insurance or government programs to pay medical bills is that the bills are too high for ordinary consumers to pay; one of the reasons that the bills are too high for ordinary consumers to pay is that we rely on insurance and government programs to pay for them.

Health care is a maddening and stupid business, and it is no wonder that Americans collectively hate insurance companies, HMOs, and hospital operators, if not physicians themselves. It is a truly goofy business—half politics (about 50 percent of all U.S. health-care spending was government, even before the PPACA) and half corporate Kafka. I am still shocked that every time I walk into a new doctor's office, I am given a clipboard and a pencil and old-fashioned paper forms to fill out—cutting-edge, nineteenth-century technology. I can open my gun safe with a thumbprint, carry all of my travel information for the benefit of Homeland Security on my scannable passport, and make a thousand-dollar purchase at the Apple Store without touching a piece of paper (Apple emails receipts), but the guy poking around my insides and prescribing me drugs is using the same technology as Charles Dickens. Very odd, that. Even more odd when you consider that every medical practice in the country has access to a very high-tech customer-tracking system—the credit-reporting network—but they use information technology to collect money, not to keep track of patients' records: twenty-first-century technology when looking after their own interests, caveman stuff when looking after yours.

You could make a very long list of what is wrong with the American health-care system, pre- or post-PPACA: Doctors and other specialists are cartelized, there is no transparency in prices, your bills are paid by third parties with economic interests antithetical to your own, interstate barriers inhibit competition between insurance carriers, there is widespread governmental price-fixing, special-interest groups dominate the major government health-care programs, and the whole mess is driving the country toward national insolvency.

American health care is great. Health-care financing is a mess.

Actual health-care products and services—from heart stents to pharmaceuticals—have for the most part followed the same better/ cheaper path as the iPhone and other bellwether products. We live in an age of miracles and wonders when it comes to health care. Within the lifetime of my father, thousands of Americans died every year from malaria, and many more from waterborne disease now associated in the American mind almost exclusively with the hot poor corners of the world. Medicated stents now make a quick and easy procedure out of much of what used to be traumatic open-heart surgery—sawing through ribs and sternums. Even AIDS, terrible as it is, is no longer necessarily a death sentence. Technology ranging from imaging hardware to pharmacological breakthroughs has radically improved the quality of life for billions of people around the world. In fact, many of the fiscal pressures on the American entitlement system are a direct consequence of the fact that the architects of those programs had no way to predict that Americans would be living so much longer in such a short period of time. When the Social Security retirement age was set at 65 years in 1935, nearly half (47 percent) of all twenty-one-year-old men would die before reaching that age. (Childhood deaths were so common that average life expectancy at birth was only 58 for men and 62 for women.) We live longer, and we have radically higher expectations about quality of life, including the quality of medical services—in other words, we have high-class problems.

During the debate over the PPACA, so-called conservatives endlessly protested that President Obama et al. were on the verge of ruining what they insisted was the greatest health-care system in the world. Republican leader John Boehner insisted that we had "the best health-care system in the world," Texas governor Rick Perry said that it was the "finest in the world," which was echoed nearly word for word by Republican Senate leader Mitch McConnell. And two out of three Republicans in the general electorate told Harris pollsters that they believed the United States to have the best health-care system in the world. One out of three Republicans believed otherwise, while Democrats had almost precisely the opposite view: Two-thirds denied that we had the best health-care system in the world, and the majority of independents agreed. The debate over the PPACA had an obvious polarizing effect. Interestingly, a 1993 *Washington Post* poll found a majority of Americans dissatisfied with the health-care system, and a 2012 poll found the same result. With the PPACA debate out of mind, the majority of Americans— and a strong majority of non-Republican Americans—report that they don't much like the health-care system. So were all of those Republicans who insisted it was the "best in the world" engaged in mere political theater, grievously out of touch, or what?

They simply are not talking about the same things. We have

great doctors, drugs, and devices—if you can afford them. And most Americans report being happy with their health insurance plans, which are for the most part a good deal—if, as in the case of those Stamford parking spaces, you can get one. Politics destroyed the housing market by trying to make housing more affordable and housing finance more accessible to people without money or credit, and for more than half a century it has been doing roughly the same thing to the health-care business. The original sin here, as often is the case, was perpetrated by the architects of the New Deal and the sincerely well-intentioned social engineers of the Franklin Roosevelt administration. Less goodhearted were the efforts of the medical associations to strangle their competition around the same time, a secondary though not insignificant event.

Is there something inherent in the structure of the health-care market that means consumers cannot pay expenses out of pocket and negotiate prices the way they would on a television or a car? In some cases, yes: If you get hit by a bus and are wheeled unconscious into the emergency room, you are not in a very good negotiating position. Likewise, if your daughter has a brain tumor, you probably are going to pay whatever it costs to have that tumor treated. But most health-care decisions are not immediate life-and-death issues. There is less reason to think that consumers cannot negotiate the price of an annual checkup or routine dental work, the inevitable cuts and scrapes in life, or preventative and diagnostic care. True, most consumers do not have a great deal of medical knowledge; most of them aren't telecommunications engineers, either, but they manage to negotiate that market just fine. But with no prices, there can be no price discrimination and no negotiation—none of the iterative social learning that characterizes our most productive enterprises.

The lack of consumer prices produces some truly odd consequences. Chad Terhune of the *Los Angeles Times* identified a clinic that charges $4,432 for a CAT scan. The clinic has a relationship with Blue Shield, which pays a negotiated price of about $2,200 for the same procedure. And the out-of-pocket price for a consumer paying cash? Only $250. But they do not advertise that price. Considering that case, Avik Roy, one of the country's leading health policy analysts, wrote: "Price transparency seems like the kind of thing that everyone should be able to rally around. But you'd be wrong. Pretty much everyone in the health-care world—other than the patient—has an interest in keeping prices opaque. . . . Most doctors and hospitals would rather not post their prices, because then patients would shop around, placing pressure on their incomes. Insurers don't like price transparency, because they view the rates they negotiate with hospitals and doctors as proprietary trade secrets that give them an advantage over their competitors. Suppliers of medical products, of course, also benefit from high prices."

We spend a ton of money on Medicare and Medicaid because medical prices are so high. And medical prices are so high in part because we spend so much money on Medicare and Medicaid. As I showed in the previous chapter, subsidizing consumption of a good while paying no attention to its production leads either to higher prices or some other kind of economic distortion. As policy analyst Doug Mataconis argues:

> For most people with health insurance, a visit to the doctor typically ends up costing no more than a small co-payment. For other medical services, some people are responsible for a typically small deductible when using insurance to pay for tests, procedures, and prescriptions. Larger charges only tend

to arise when, for some reason, an individual ends up receiving care from an institution or physician that isn't part of the insurance network, although with most large insurance networks like Blue Cross/Blue Shield that seems to be much less of an issue than it used to be. For the typical person in a typical year, though, there's almost no thought given to the cost of a medical procedure (why not go to the doctor for those sniffles when it only costs you a $10 co-pay?).

It didn't always work this way. For a long time, health insurance, including insurance provided through employers, typically only covered major medical procedures and hospitalization (I remember terms like "major medical" and "hospitalization" being used to describe health insurance as late as the 1970s). Over the years, though, insurance has come to cover more and more "routine" medical expenses, and consumers have become more and more unaware of the actual cost of their health care, to the point where now just 12% of health care costs are paid directly by consumers.

When consumers are insulated from the cost of a good or service, they aren't going to take the price of that good or service into account when deciding whether or not to purchase it, which means that the normal supply-demand price mechanism isn't going to work. In the long run, this means prices will go up.

Insurance companies do have an incentive to keep prices down, but they have other, more effective cost-cutting methods: namely, dumping subscribers who are sick or who are likely to get sick, or denying coverage completely for procedures that are likely to be needed. Combined with a relative lack of competition among insurance companies and medical providers, that ensures a sick market.

What if we treated health care like a normal good?

Imagine that, some years in the future, a firm called LifeCorp began marketing an amazing new product: a pill called Health, which would ensure that you would remain in perfect health for approximately the next sixty years, at which point the effects of the drug would wear off and could not be replicated with a second dose. You might die in a car wreck or be strangled to death by somebody's jealous husband, but you would never catch a cold, contract cancer, or suffer from diabetes, and would be immune to everything from Alzheimer's to AIDS. You could smoke and drink and eat all you liked without ever worrying about emphysema, liver problems, or obesity. There are, of course, some restrictions: Health won't cure a serious disease you already have, and its effectiveness diminishes the later in life you take it—an eighteen-year-old or a twenty-one-year-old would get the full sixty years protection, but a forty-year-old would get less, say thirty-five to forty years. Imagine that the single pill was very expensive—say, the equivalent of $100,000 in today's money. That price tag might look shocking, but when you consider that you'd never need health insurance covering anything other than accidents, that you'd never pay a doctor's bill or a prescription-drug copay, and—most important—that you'd never have to worry about any of that, it would probably be a pretty good deal. That $100,000 might seem like a lot for a single pill, but it would not be very much for a house and so, as with houses, many people would finance their once-in-a-lifetime dose of Health over twenty or forty years. LifeCorp, like a car dealership, is happy to let you buy now and pay later. Banks begin to offer special Health-financing plans: You make a small down payment on or about your eighteenth birthday and then pay off your Health over time. Wealthy parents give their children Health for a high school graduation present. Poor parents aspire to do so.

But LifeCorp has competitors, and one of them introduces a product, Salubrius, offering benefits identical to those of Health, but a lot cheaper—only $55,000—and a little less long-lasting: fifty years instead of sixty years. LifeCorp, determined to defend its market share, hits back with two products: HealthPro and HealthMax. HealthPro is the entry-level product, undercutting Salubrius by $5,000 but offering only forty years of protection. At the other end of the market, HealthMax, an amazing breakthrough, offers an astounding hundred years of protection at a steep price: $1 million.

Given that market of amazing, health-protecting drugs, people would be forced to make some economic decisions: How to calculate the trade-off between years of health protection and up-front costs? How much to worry about the relatively small possibility of contracting a fatal disease before age eighteen? Do I really even want to live to be more than 118 years old, even if I'm in perfect health? What if I have two children about to turn eighteen but can only afford a single prescription? I took HealthMax when I was twenty but my fiancée, now thirty-two, has never had one of these miracle prescriptions—what should we do?

And while the microeconomic questions might be complicated, the macroeconomic questions would be even hairier. As these drugs become better and cheaper over time (because they are normal marketplace products) and disease and sickness become a problem belonging almost uniquely to the poor, there might be a social stigma attached to sickness—but, at the same time, we'd be free to concentrate all of our considerable health-care resources on those who need them. So what should we do? How does the fact that the very wealthy can expect to be considerably healthier for a longer period of time than those of more modest means affect social cohesion and social mobility? (And what will happen to all the poor oncologists and health insurance executives, now out of work? Will they be able to afford Health?)

We would have to make many of the same decisions we have to make regarding health care today. We all know that we eventually will get sick and die—if we're lucky. If we're unlucky, we'll crash our motorcycles or walk down the wrong block in Detroit. We have to in effect ration our health care, deciding how much we're willing to pay for what sort of protection, just like we do with every other product and service we consume. In short, although we would be radically better off than we are today, many of the underlying sources of our anxiety about health care would remain unchanged. Scarcity is real, and no scarcity is more intractable than the scarcity of lifetime. We are not going to live forever, and the main question of health care is what happens between now and the time we die. As usual, the question is: Who plans for whom?

One of the main problems with health-care reform is ideological rather than economic: The wealthy have access to more and better goods and services than the poor do—that is the definition of "wealthy"—but there is a very strong current in politics that objects to this when it comes to health care. Rather than focus on improving the quality and price of goods and services across the marketplace to the benefit of rich and poor alike, there has been a great deal of emphasis on equalizing the market position of the rich and the poor. This does not serve anybody's interests, least of all those of the poor, who in many cases would be better served by putting resources into assistance not related to health care. As Cowen argues: "Trying to equalize health-care consumption hurts the poor, since most feasible policies to do this take away cash from the poor, either directly or through the operation of tax incidence. We need to accept the principle that sometimes poor people will die just because they are poor. Some of you don't like the sound of that, but we already let the wealthy enjoy all sorts of other goods—most importantly status—which lengthen their lives and which the poor enjoy to a much lesser degree. We shouldn't screw up our health-care institutions by being determined to fight inegalitarian principles for one very select set of factors which determine health-care outcomes."

There are many volumes to be written on the history of what went wrong with American health care, but here is a short and very simplified version: The Roosevelt administration began imposing central planning on broad swathes of the U.S. economy in the 1930s, but in an effort to escape the Great Depression and to prepare the country for war. One of the things the administration did was to impose wage and price controls, and it was ruthless about enforcing them. The great newspaperman R. C. Hoiles, who had been a fierce critic of President Roosevelt's creation of the Japanese internment camps, was fined a thousand dollars—not for cutting salaries but for giving his employees an unapproved raise. With the war on, businesses had to compete ruthlessly for good employees, but the wage controls prevented them from luring workers with higher pay. (Seriously—through a depression and the onset of a world war, the Roosevelt administration was cracking down on employers for paying people too much.) Thus was born the fringe benefit: company cars, expense accounts, and, most popular, employer-sponsored health insurance plans. Because these benefits were not considered income per se, payments made by employers for health insurance did not come under the income tax, a situation that persists to this day. Over time, that produced a truly odd and destructive economic arrangement: The company store has been abolished everywhere except in health insurance. That creates perverse incentives on both sides. The insurance company is not beholden to the consumer, but to the consumer's employer: Apple has to work hard to keep me happy to keep my business, but Aetna only has to be good enough that it's not worth it to my employer to switch to another provider. And while my employer may value me, it also values its bottom line. As Milton Friedman once observed, there are four ways to spend money: 1) Spend your own money on yourself; 2) spend your own money on somebody else; 3) spend somebody else's money on yourself; 4) spend somebody else's money on somebody else. When it comes to health care, your employer does No. 2 and the government does No. 4. Under No. 2, you have a very strong incentive to pay attention to price but less incentive to pay attention to quality, whereas under No. 4 you have no incentive to pay attention to price or quality. (Under No. 1, which prevails in most markets, you have a very strong incentive to pay attention to both price and quality—in other words, to value.)

A second perverse incentive is that at the top end of the tax range, the tax-free status of health benefits means that $1 diverted from taxable salary buys about $1.50 in benefits. As your income goes up, you have an ever-more-powerful incentive to take your compensation in the form of health benefits rather than in cash. (This trend is compounded by the fact that both your income and your health-care consumption tend to go up as you get older.) While the first set of perverse incentives gives employers a reason to lowball the quality of coverage for all but the most highly paid employees, the second set of perverse incentives tends to drive up prices.

The question is not what to do about health care, but what to do about insurance. As with voluntary and nonpolitical models of education (Harvard, homeschooling), we have in our historical experience some models of insurance that are relevant to our present straits. While it would not make sense to replicate them in every particular, they illustrate some principles that should guide our thinking.

Before the New Deal, a surprisingly large number of Americans were covered by social insurance plans—plans that existed entirely outside the sphere of formal politics. These programs offered a surprising array of services: life insurance, hospitalization, medical benefits covering everything from doctors' fees and hospital charges to wages lost due to illness or injury, survivors benefits, old-age pensions, and even care at retirement homes. And these were not programs for the rich, but for the working class and the poor: Their members were disproportionately low-income laborers, immigrants, and African-Americans. They were administered on a nonprofit, voluntary, peer-to-peer basis by community associations of a sort that have, unfortunately, all but disappeared, and the resurrection of which would offer a very attractive alternative to the declining entitlement state. Familiar fraternal organizations such as the Masons, the Elks Lodge, and the Odd Fellows, together with smaller groups and organizations specific to particular ethnic and immigrant populations, included an astonishing number of Americans in the first half of the twentieth century: About one in three Americans over the age of twenty-one belonged to such groups; that number, however, understates their prevalence, since many of those members were the heads of households whose wives and children were covered by the social insurance policies they offered. In large cities such as Baltimore and Philadelphia, about 98 percent of adult African-Americans carried insurance through fraternal associations such as the Colored Knights of Pythias. At least 12 percent of adult white men belonged to the Masons alone. W. E. B. DuBois estimated that at least 70 percent of the residents of the black section of Philadelphia belonged to fraternal lodges, mutual aid societies, or self-help insurance programs. The benefits were not particularly generous by contemporary standards, but consider that an African-American man born in 2001 has an average life expectancy of less than sixty-five years—meaning that a majority of black men will not live long enough to collect a dime in Social Security or Medicare benefits, though they will spend a lifetime paying taxes to support the programs. (The programs historically have been a much better deal for white women, the longest-lived large demographic group in the United States. Americans of Okinawan origin make out like bandits, on average.)

Fraternal lodges and other mutual aid societies secured medical benefits for their members on a model that came to be known as "lodge practice." In short, the groups would contract with a doctor or a group of doctors, paying a fixed sum each year (or quarterly) for each beneficiary in the organization. Those payments entitled members to office visits and house calls covering the full range of services that doctors offered. (There were some exceptions: Many of the mutual aid policies declined to cover venereal disease or health problems resulting from excessive drinking. To this day, some life insurance policies revoke benefits in deaths in which alcohol was a primary causal factor.) Because these organizations often had hundreds of members, they could entice doctors with contracts that cost members as little as one dollar a year. Unsurprisingly, this arrangement was most attractive to new doctors fresh out of medical school; by contracting with a lodge (or a number of lodges) they could immediately establish a practice that might have taken years to develop otherwise. In his fascinating study of fraternal societies, historian David Beito found that on New York City's Lower East

Side—a very poor community in the early twentieth century—more than five hundred doctors had contracts with local Jewish lodges alone. The Irish, the Italians, the Poles, and other immigrant groups had similar arrangements. Beito writes:

> This method bore more than a faint resemblance to a modern health maintenance organization. It appealed in particular to younger doctors eager to establish a clientele or elderly doctors seeking a part-time practice. In later years, Samuel Silverberg, a lodge doctor during this period, recalled that the "society would pay me a certain amount for coverage for a certain number of patients—fifty cents for every single member every three months, seventy-five cents or a dollar for a family. Every member had a right to come to my office and ask me to call at his house. . . . The society member would recommend the doctor to his friends, and that way you could build up a practice. But it was hard, lots of running up and down tenement stairs."

If you have ever heard a contemporary doctor complain about dealing with an insurance company, Medicare, or Medicaid, you might be forgiven for suspecting that he'd be willing to forgo the Stairmaster and get some real-world exercise in exchange for being paid directly and predictably, with a minimum of outside bureaucratic interference.

What is remarkable about the mutual aid society is that it consisted for the most part of poor people insuring poor people, without the benefit of paternalistic charity or paternalistic government. The peer-to-peer model had a number of advantages: Beneficiaries were less likely to abuse their benefits, because they were dealing with their friends and neighbors rather than with some faceless corporation with interests at odds with their own. Lodge members could use gentle forms of persuasion, such as negative gossip, to police malingerers, and here again reputation proves a very effective alternative to outright coercion: A lodge member known to have cheated his friends and neighbors would have a very hard time acquiring coverage from another lodge, or even membership in that lodge. Neighboring is serious business. These social and communal ties are powerful things, probably more important than narrow economic incentives—but those were in place as well: Because society members often had life insurance and medical benefits through the same society—not to mention funeral plans or the expectation that they or a loved one would spend their final years in a society-run retirement home—they had very good reasons to regard their own economic well-being as closely aligned with that of the society.

When it comes to insurance, there is of course great power in numbers. The employees of Coca-Cola, for example, routinely report high levels of satisfaction with their health-care plans. In fact, Coca-Cola employees rate their benefits more highly than they do their senior management. And Coca-Cola can demand very good health coverage for its employees: There are about 150,000 of them. No insurance executive wants to be the guy who blew the Coke account. But what about people who do not work for Coca-Cola or Procter & Gamble or another corporate titan? Consider that there are about as many freelance writers in the United States as there are Coca-Cola employees. There are 500,000 members of the NAACP, 20 million college students, and 77 million Catholics. The National Model Railroad Association has more members than the pharmaceutical giant Amgen has employees—and the pocket-protector set in Amgen's laboratories boasts of very good health benefits.

The U.S. Catholic bishops informally (and sometimes quasi-formally) lobbied for the passage of the PPACA—and then complained bitterly when the same Leviathan they'd gotten into bed with decided to force Catholic institutions to buy insurance paying for services they object to on moral grounds, such as abortifacient drugs. Imagine how much better things would have gone if instead of lobbying the government for a coercive, one-size-fits-all solution to the very real health-care problems facing the United States, the Catholic Church had gotten into the mutual-aid insurance business itself. If the 150,000 employees of Coca-Cola are a big enough buying bloc to negotiate a great deal for themselves, how much better could the 77 million Catholics in the United States have done—especially with a nonprofit provider made up of the beneficiaries themselves? If such a thing were organized at the diocesan or parish level, it would replicate many of the social benefits associated with the old fraternal model of self-insurance while also availing itself of the benefits of the church's awesome head count.

Markets work, the free-marketers insist, and they do—but in a great many instances, they work even better in situations in which narrow economic self-interest is not the only motivating factor. In my home church in New York City, families know each other. They worship together and socialize together. Their children in many cases go to school together and play together. As it happens, many of the people I work with attend the same church, and the father confessor knows things about me that my poor parents were never burdened with knowing. Our social and community ties are deep and—that word again!—complex. The disincentive to abuse or overuse insurance benefits offered in that context is very strong. Likewise, given the charitable nature of the institution, the fact that better-off members would in effect subsidize worse-off members would be taken as a matter of course, and I'd intensely prefer dealing with people I know and care about—and who know and care about me—when I am in a vulnerable position than the fine folks at Acme Insurance Faceless Conglomerate Inc.

Markets work better when there is trust, and when transactions take place in the context of ongoing relationships with many opportunities for repeated interaction. This is true even in the most ruthless of marketplaces: Wall Street. There was a time when the two most dreaded letters in the world of Wall Street were "DK." That stands for "Don't Know," and to DK somebody maliciously is one of the worst offenses you can commit on Wall Street. A malicious DK takes place when a trader agrees to a particular transaction and then denies ever having agreed to it if the trade turns out to be a loser for him—he says, "I don't know the trade." There are legitimate DKs—sometimes there is legitimate disagreement about the terms of a deal—but there are also DKs called just to avoid a losing transaction. Pulling an unwarranted DK can save a trader from a loss, but it can also end his career: The world of Wall Street is global, but it is, ironically, not that big a world, and traders have to do a lot of repeat business with the same counterparties. If a major investment house refuses to do business with you in retaliation for a malicious DK, you can find yourself out of work.

Improvements in information technology have taken some of the uncertainty out of Wall Street financial transactions—and they have created new models of peer-to-peer finance as well. The website Kickstarter began as a way for fans to support the work of musicians and other artists, for instance by kicking in a small amount of money to support the recording of a new album in exchange for receiving a copy of the work upon its completion. But it quickly grew into a powerful entrepreneurial engine for everything from works of literature to video games and consumer electronics. Kickstarter created a new kind of financial transaction, one that has characteristics of both an investment and a purchase. Patrons expect to receive the work or the product they have supported, but of course not every entrepreneurial endeavor comes to successful fruition, so there is an element of uncertainty. Under Kickstarter's policies, entrepreneurs who fail to deliver their products are supposed to give refunds to their patrons, but of course there are expenses incurred when attempting to develop a product, and sometimes the money isn't there. Other than its stated policy, Kickstarter has no enforcement mechanism to ensure that these refunds happen—in fact, the site doesn't even have a tool for handling refunds, which mostly have been executed through PayPal. Kickstarter is a trust-based system, and founder Yancey Strickler says that the cooperative nature of the enterprise has made entrepreneurs conscientious about delivering and patrons patient about delays and setbacks. "By creating a system where it's just a series of open and direct exchanges between people with ideas and projects, and people interested in supporting them," Strickler told NPR, "you have everyone on the same page, and everyone understanding what's going on." And these are not small-time deals: Kickstarter patrons have financed successful multimillion-dollar projects.

Recently, there have been some stirrings suggesting a renewal of the self-help/mutual-aid model of health care. The Old Order Amish set up a church fund in the 1960s to formalize its process for helping church members share the burdens of medical costs. Inspired by that example, dozens of mostly Christian organizations have begun to establish "health-care-sharing ministries" for distributing medical costs. Like the old mutual-aid societies, these organizations are a good deal nosier than your average insurance company (most insist on adherence to a "biblical lifestyle," meaning no drugs or nonmarital sex, etc.), and they enforce norms by publishing the names of aid recipients and the amount of aid received. One organization, Samaritan Ministries, describes the process:

> Each month there is a fixed amount of shares available from members that will be sent to meet needs. The amount of needs in a given month may fluctuate and be greater or less than the shares available.
>
> When there are more shares available than amount of needs submitted for a month, needs already received for the following month will be shared a month early. If there is still a surplus of share money when it is time to prepare the monthly newsletter mailing, the share amount for that month will be reduced to the amount needed. The most recent time this happened was in October 2008, when assigned share amounts were reduced by 15 percent.
>
> In months when more needs are submitted than the amount of share money available, we use a process we call prorating. For example, if $1,000,000 in publishable needs are submitted, but there is only $900,000 in share money available, then only 90 percent of each need will be published.
>
> If there is extra share money available the following month, the surplus will be used to help with the prorated needs. The other members are also encouraged to give additional gifts, if they are able. In addition, many members whose needs have been prorated have found that their health care providers will reduce their charges to the prorated amounts, or the members may receive additional money from unexpected sources. God has many ways of providing.

In fifteen years of ministry, we've found that even prorated needs are met through generous extra giving and through the many other ways in which God provides.

About those "biblical lifestyles." These organizations are for the most part conservative and Protestant, though there is no reason that a group of lesbian atheists or liberal Muslims could not set up such an organization. In the case of traditional conservative groups, one assumes that things like abortion or sex-change operations would not be covered, and this decision should be entirely uncontroversial in the case of purely voluntary organizations—another thing that makes them importantly different from political health-care programs. As an aside, one of the interesting aspects of this model of self-help is that it offers a chance to put to the test certain claims by social conservatives regarding tradition, sexuality, and family life. If their claims are substantially true—that traditional family arrangements produce happier, healthier, better-adjusted people—then that advantage should show up in the financial data of these lifestyle-homogeneous self-insurance organizations. Christian traditionalists should welcome the opportunities to put their social theories to the test of the marketplace, as should their secularist tormentors.

The Christian health-sharing ministries are not nearly as financially or technologically sophisticated as they should be, but they are a step in the right direction. Combining the distributed, peer-to-peer model of cooperation exemplified by Kickstarter and similar online ventures with the old-fashioned virtues of self-reliance and community cohesion exemplified by the fraternal-insurance societies provides a promising model for replacing our dysfunctional health insurance system with something more humane, flexible, and efficient. And we have a tool available to us that the Masons and the Elks Lodge did not: Rigorously engineered modern actuarial practices can make cooperative insurance projects orders of magnitude more efficient than they were in the 1930s. The main obstacle standing in the way is, as usual, politics: Insurance is part of the banking and finance world, which—contrary to a decade's worth of uninformed commentary to the contrary—is one of the most highly regulated industries in the developed world. The model-railroad guys probably couldn't set up a cooperative insurance society if they wanted to. But deregulation alone will not cause better insurance institutions to magically spring into existence ex nihilo. That will require innovation and leadership, especially from large, well-established voluntary institutions. I didn't choose the Catholic Church as an example lightly: The bishops are precisely the sort of civil-society leaders who should be out front on these issues. So should the Human Rights Campaign and the American Family Association—and the Masons and the Elks are still around, too, for that matter. There have been some efforts made in this direction, notably by the Freelancers Union, an organization of self-employed people, mostly working in the creative occupations. Unfortunately, therein lies a cautionary tale as well: The Freelancers Union was coopted by politics when it agreed to accept $174 million in government funding under the PPACA, along with millions more in state and local subsidies. Predictably, the pursuit of government money has led the organization away from pursuing innovative collaborative channels of action and deeper into the morass of politics.

But if somebody could remind His Eminence Timothy Cardinal Dolan that millions of Irish-Americans, Polish-Americans, and Italian-Americans, almost exclusively Catholic, used to within living memory take care of themselves and their neighbors—being their brothers' keepers, feeding the hungry, housing the homeless, providing for orphans and widows, the whole enchilada—without any help from the political powers (which is to say, without rendering *too much* unto Caesar), and maybe introduce him to Kickstarter, he might not have to worry too much about Washington telling him that he has to pay for mifepristone on Monday after sermonizing against it on Sunday. And the Secular Coalition for America can buy whatever kind of insurance it wants, too—and nobody has to fight about it.

CHAPTER 6

Captive Minds: The Politics of
the Education Cartel

I n the American context, there probably is no better example of the
contrast between the world of the iPhone (the world that works)
and the world of politics (the world that doesn't work) than the public school system. Consider the cell phone in your pocket, which
gets better and cheaper every year, and the public school down the
street, which gets more expensive and less functional every year. The
contrast is striking. There is a temptation to think of the difference
as being merely technological: We are used to rapid improvements
in the quality and affordability of gadgets and gear. But measured
against practically any other product of the private economy—from
bread and butter to banking services and airline travel—the contrast
is substantially the same: lower prices and higher quality in the private economy, the opposite in the schools. When you have learned
why that is, then you will know why the end of politics is an end very
much to be desired.

The main obstacle to applying a consumer product model to the
public schools is that the education establishment operates in a state
of confusion that would be comical if its consequences were not so

very dire: It has mistaken its *customers* for its *product*. The American public education establishment operates under a nationalistic nineteenth-century ideology that, like most of the welfare state, has its roots in Otto von Bismarck's imperial Germany and is informed by notions about economic central planning that have long been discredited among most professional economists. A functional, market-based education system would properly recognize that its *customers* are students and that its *products* are various kinds of education, ranging from classical liberal arts studies to forms of specific occupational training. Being political institutions, the schools operate under the theory that their *customer* is the State—or "society" at large—and that their *product* is a national workforce, tailored to meet national needs—which is to say, political needs. Government resembles business in many ways, an important one being that the man who writes the check gives orders to the man who accepts it in all circumstances (except, of course, for the man who writes a check with a gun to his head, that is, the taxpayer).

The State, under this theory, requires particular kinds of workers. In Bismarck's day, that meant above all highly trained technocrats to staff the growing bureaucratic and administrative machinery of the totalitarian state, but also skilled workers for the rapidly developing German industrial economy. In our own time, those two mandates remain the schools' uppermost priorities, though we use more democratic language to speak about the former (preparing students to be "good citizens," meaning easily governed taxpayers) and in most circumstances emphasize the latter. The model is the factory engaged in the mass production of industrial goods. Students are to be turned out like widgets to meet the needs of the only customer who matters: the one who pays the bills. It is for this reason that all serious education reform programs must put private citizens—

students and their families—in charge of appropriating education funds, rather than political bodies. And it is for the same reason that the education establishment, notably the teachers' unions but also administrators and most career education professionals, is red in tooth and claw in its opposition to removing political controls from education dollars.

The Obama administration tellingly describes its guiding educational principles in terms that cast students as national resources to be deployed serving the interests of the State: "Providing a high-quality education for all children is critical to America's economic future. Our nation's economic competitiveness and the path to the American Dream depend on providing every child with an education that will enable them to succeed in a global economy that is predicated on knowledge and innovation. President Obama is committed to providing every child access to a complete and competitive education, from cradle through career. President Obama will reform America's public schools to deliver a twenty-first-century education that will prepare all children for success in the new global workplace." Even in this embarrassing specimen of political boilerplate, we can discover the underlying ideology. The main thing to notice is that the national interest ("America's economic future," "our nation's economic competitiveness") comes first, while the individual's interest ("the path to the American Dream") is tacked on as an afterthought. The Obama administration is by no means unique in this regard. Every administration describes education in the same language, because etatist ideologies are by their nature bipartisan, Democrats and Republicans being two branches of the same political enterprise.

The persistence of this rhetoric is not trivial. If you listen, the State will tell you what it really wants and what it really intends, in spite of the political establishment's best efforts to obscure the facts. The roots of this ideology run very deep. The nineteenth-century American education reformer and progressive thinker Calvin Stowe argued explicitly for military-style compulsion in the matter of schooling: "If a regard to the public safety makes it right for a government to compel the citizens to do military duty when the country is invaded, the same reason authorizes the government to compel them to provide for the education of their children. . . . A man has no more right to endanger the state by throwing upon it a family of ignorant and vicious children, than he has to give admission to the spies of an invading army." Stowe was a critical advocate of bringing the Prussian model of education to the United States, and the distinctively German character of the Prussian ideology can be traced back at least as far as to Martin Luther, who wrote in a very similar vein: "I maintain that the civil authorities are under obligation to compel the people to send their children to school. . . . If the government can compel such citizens as are fit for military service to bear spear and rifle, to mount ramparts, and perform other martial duties in time of war, how much more has it a right to the people to send their children to school, because in this case we are warring with the devil, whose object it is secretly to exhaust our cities and principalities."

Lest the reader think it fanciful to trace the philosophical underpinnings of compulsory schooling back so far, consider that our nation's first compulsory-education law, adopted during the Puritan era, was called, evocatively, the "Old Deluder Satan Law" of 1647. Being much more succinct than the No Child Left Behind Act, it reads:

It being one chief project of that old deluder, Satan, to keep men from the knowledge of the Scriptures, as in former times by keeping them in an unknown tongue, so in these latter times by persuading from the use of tongues, that so that at least the true sense and meaning of the original might be clouded and corrupted with false glosses of saint-seeming deceivers; and to the end that learning may not be buried in the grave of our forefathers, in church and commonwealth, the Lord assisting our endeavors. It is therefore ordered that every township in this jurisdiction, after the Lord hath increased them to fifty households shall forthwith appoint one within their town to teach all such children as shall resort to him to write and read, whose wages shall be paid either by the parents or masters of such children, or by the inhabitants in general, by way of supply, as the major part of those that order the prudentials of the town shall appoint; provided those that send their children be not oppressed by paying much more than they can have them taught for in other towns. And it is further ordered, that when any town shall increase to the number of one hundred families or householders, they shall set up a grammar school, the master thereof being able to instruct youth so far as they may be fitted for the university, provided that if any town neglect the performance hereof above one year that every such town shall pay 5 pounds to the next school till they shall perform this order.

The anti-Catholic assumptions of the law (the bit about keeping the scriptures in an unknown tongue would have pressed Puritan buttons) was characteristic of English nationalism during and after the Reformation, before "national competitiveness" became the official state religion worldwide.

So, at first it was God who needed an educated citizenry, then

God's deputy, the king, ruling by divine right, then the more quotidian secular-nationalist autocrat, and today those meaningless
aggregates "our nation" and "the economy," all of which in political reality amount to the same thing. Given that the modern liberal
state, like its royal and imperial ancestors, recognizes no meaningful distinction between the State, the nation, the economy, etc., it is
not in the least surprising that the ideology of compulsory education has survived very much intact. It is therefore easy to answer
the question, "Why does the education system not do a better job
of serving our students' interests?" The answer: *Because it is not designed to.* It is designed to serve the interests of the State.

The State's interests in education are complex and sometimes incompatible with one another. Some of those interests are, in fact,
the State's publicly stated interests: developing responsible citizens,
providing skilled labor to economic enterprises, etc. Those goals are
legitimate and well-intended, though our system does a remarkably
poor job of achieving them. The nation's best technological, scientific, and financial firms are increasingly compelled to go abroad for
top-level talent, and employers represented by the U.S. Chamber of
Commerce complain constantly about the poor quality of American high school graduates and, increasingly, of those with college
degrees. Our nation's adult illiteracy rate (the data are famously intractable, but the National Center for Education Statistics estimates
that 14 percent of American adults are illiterate or near-illiterate,
and a total of 29 percent have very low levels of literacy), our high
school graduates' knowledge of American civic institutions and history, their performance in science and mathematics, etc., suggest
that the system is performing poorly.

The State's other educational interests are rarely if ever stated,
and it is critical to understand them if we are to understand the

nature of the education system and the sources of its failures. Those interests are complex and varied. They include, but are not limited to: facilitating the regimentation of political and economic life (explicitly in the case of Bismarck's Germany and contemporary China, implicitly in the United States); engaging in ideological indoctrination; providing relatively high-wage, secure, noncompetitive employment for members of the political class; and cultivating citizens' habits of acquiescence to administrative discipline early in life. It is not coincidental that as the United States continues to commit extraordinary levels of economic and political resources to public schools and prisons, the two have begun to resemble one another to a remarkable extent. (University of Texas alumni such as myself are acutely aware that the father of Texas's public school funding system, Governor Beauford H. Jester, has two major public facilities named for him: the famous Jester Center dormitory, a particularly hideous example of Brutalist penal architecture adopted for non-penitentiary use, and the comparatively bucolic Jester Prison Farm.) A few years back, I had cause to visit a jail in rural Kentucky and noted that it had considerably less security in place than a typical New York City public school, the latter having armed police, metal detectors, surveillance cameras, and the like.

Understood properly, the standard municipal public school system in the United States is the State in miniature. Like all states, it has three defining characteristics, being a 1) regional 2) monopoly 3) on violence. You may not be accustomed to thinking of your local public school as a practitioner of violence, but, like all political institutions, it is built upon a foundation of force. The violence of the school system is of a particularly brutal kind: Whereas most instantiations of the State demand only that victims acquiesce to the expropriation of their income and assets, the public school system seizes the victim himself, and practically all Americans spend the better part of their first two decades of life as government property, limited-purpose chattels whose attendance at government schools is compulsory. That compulsion is enforced more strongly even than is the compulsory attendance of soldiers to their duties: A soldier who abandons his post may be imprisoned, but a mother who refuses to cooperate with compulsory-schooling rules may, in addition to being imprisoned, have her children taken away from her and her parental rights legally terminated. If we attempted to do such a thing to a violent felon, it almost certainly would be considered cruel and unusual punishment—indeed, it would hardly occur to us to punish most criminal wrongdoers in the way we punish families that, for whatever reason, resist the compulsion to attend government schools or government-approved alternatives.

In the United States, the public schools are the most perfect example of etatism to be found in civilian life. Their form of economic organization is socialism: The government generally owns the means of production, the workers in the education factories are government employees, and there is no private market. The existence of private schools does not obviate that lattermost fact. Though only a vanishingly small number of Americans attend them, the private schools serve a critical political function that is necessary to the maintenance of the broader government-school regime and therefore are most accurately considered a part of the public school system, not an alternative to it. The political function of private schools is to give the wealthy and the politically powerful ready alternatives to the dysfunctional monopoly of school systems, ensuring that the very parties who are best positioned to achieve meaningful reform of the government schools are those who have the least incentive to do so, and that those who suffer the worst of the public schools' dysfunction are those who have the least economic or political ability to do anything about it. There is a kind of genius at work in that: Practically no one objects to the fact that the wealthy and the politically powerful exempt themselves and their children from the public school monopoly. It is practically a ritual for the greatest public school champions in Washington to enroll their own children at Sidwell Friends, as the Obamas did and the Clintons before them. It is only when reforms threaten to give the poor and those without political influence access to alternatives that the State begins to insist that its monopoly must be enforced. At the very moment Barack Obama was enrolling his children at Sidwell Friends, he was maneuvering to eliminate the D.C. Hope Scholarship program, a very popular initiative that gave thousands of uniformly poor and mostly black inner-city Washington students alternatives to what are some of the least effective, not to mention most dangerous, public schools in the country. When it comes to presidential families, the decision to enroll children in private schools often is presented as an issue of security or privacy, but no such concerns explain the fact that nearly half of public school teachers in Philadelphia enroll their own children in private schools.

The local public school authorities must be relieved that they do. It is easy of course to imagine that if President Obama were to have enrolled his children in a typical Washington public school and to have been scandalized by the conditions that persisted within, then those schools would have been changed. Presidents have that kind of power. But it is not presidents alone, or even presidents mainly, who wield such influence. The upper-middle to upper classes collectively enjoy the ability to deeply change a large political enterprise. (If you wish to test this hypothesis, I suggest making a 911 police call from Wall Street, where there is practically no street-level crime—the crime there being of a distinctly quiet variety—and then another from the South Bronx, and time the responses.) Another way of saying this is that if the twenty-six thousand teachers, administrators, and staff of the School District of Philadelphia were unhappy with the state of the city's schools, then they would be precisely the sort of people who could change them. The administrative elite command multimillion-dollar compensation contracts, while the teachers earn well more than the city's median wage and their unions form an important political constituency. They are, in other words, precisely the kind of economic and political elite that has the power to enact real reform. But they do not want to. The monopoly arrangement ensures not only that relatively little is expected from them and that they are in effect protected from all accountability, but also that they earn enough money to protect their own children from the system they have created.

Likewise, the private schools provide a kind of safety valve for the more committed and energetic parents who might otherwise be inclined to seek reform in the public schools. If one is motivated mainly by concern for one's own children, then the more effective route is to forgo launching a lengthy, arduous, and expensive campaign to reform the public schools—an undertaking in which success would be far from certain—and simply to remove one's own family from the scene by switching to private schools. It is for this reason that, under current practices, the private schools are more accurately considered an extension of the government-school monopoly rather than an alternative to it. The importance of that arrangement is amplified by the fact that the government schools enjoy almost everywhere an absolute monopoly on the fundamental aspect of their enterprise: the collection of tax revenues. It is of little consequence to the public school authorities if a relatively small number of students are educated outside of the cartel, so long as the authorities enjoy an uncontested monopoly on tax receipts, which ensures that they are paid both for those students they educate and for those educated elsewhere. With a market that is literally captive, ensured revenue with no meaningful accountability for performance, above-market compensation rates, heavy political protection from emergent competitors, and the biggest lobbying budget in Washington, the public schools have a setup that no robber baron or mafioso would have dared to dream of—and summers off, to boot.

Given our maxim—Reality Is Not Optional—and our promise that we will understand political organizations by analyzing what they do rather than what they say they intend to do, the public schools are best characterized as a wealth-transfer program in which resources are taken from renters (ranging from very poor Section 8 apartment dwellers to wealthy commercial enterprises), landlords, and homeowners, with the poor paying a disproportionately high rate (because they tend to rent rather than to own homes, meaning that they are paying their landlords' taxes at the commercial-property rate without the benefits and tax deductions enjoyed by homeowners). This money is then given to a group of largely female and white, upper-middle-class college graduates with professional credentials. The poor, the black, and the Hispanic are the worst served by the system, while the elite exits through the escape hatch to private schools. That this is done in the name of fairness, democratic idealism, equality, social justice, and other such high-minded miasmas suggests a cynicism that is startling in its depth and subtlety.

This is a remarkably sophisticated con, and it is especially impressive considering the relatively low intellectual caliber of the people in charge of the public school system. Decades' worth of research has shown that education majors have the lowest scores on the SAT and other standardized tests of any group of college graduates—yet students taking education classes receive, strangely enough, the highest college grades, which would seem to be evidence of massive grade inflation. That grade inflation continues throughout the public schools themselves, in which teachers receive "overwhelmingly positive evaluations," according to a report from the New Teacher Project. As Cory Koedel of the University of Missouri puts it: "Grades . . . play an important filtering role in most academic departments, deterring students with limited skills or with skills poorly matched to the discipline. Grades do not appear to play such a role in education departments." To say the least. The consequences of that fact are everywhere to be seen. Koedel again: "A superintendent asked a school principal to tell him how many of her teachers were performing well. The principal replied that they were all performing well. Puzzled, the superintendent reminded her that the vast majority of the children at the school were not reading even within a year of grade level, and he asked the question again. The principal's response was unchanged. He then asked the principal which of the teachers at her school would be suitable to teach her own granddaughter. She replied, 'Well, if that's the bar, then none of them.'"

Such is the way of politics. What might a market-based system look like? What might we expect from a system that can distinguish its customers from its product?

To begin with, there would be no system per se, and certainly no system that comprises 90-odd percent of the students. Indeed, it is a mark of the absurdity of our current thinking that we imagine a single form of K–12 education is appropriate for nearly every child in the country—we have nine hundred kinds of shampoo, and one outdated, nineteenth-century model of schooling. Rather than a unified national education regime, we should expect to see in education—as in telecommunications, transportation, food, housing, banking and finance, and other normal products—a diversity of systems reflecting the diversity of the learning population, each serving a specific customer base, each oriented toward different outcomes. "Education" is, after all, a cumbrously broad term. Teaching thirteen-year-olds Latin is not very much like teaching two-year-olds to read or teaching twenty-two-year-olds to be HVAC technicians or litigators or teaching forty-year-olds to fabricate superconductors. But all of these systems would have some things in common. All would recognize the right of Exit—the right for consumers whose needs are not being served to take their business and their money to different providers. All would be, therefore, competitive.

We cannot design a perfect education system for today, much less one that will still be perfect twenty years from now, any more than Alexander Graham Bell could have designed an iPhone, or any more than Steve Jobs could have designed a telephone that would serve the needs of consumers fifty years from now. What we can do is create the conditions under which such educational products may emerge. Spontaneous orders can evolve and adapt, while preconstructed systems cannot.

The first step toward creating the conditions for these spontaneous orders to emerge is, as noted above, to sever the link between politics and educational funding. This need not be a radical or disruptive development—indeed, it could, and very likely will, happen while the public school system continues to go about its dysfunctional business. It does not necessitate the privatization of the educational system en masse and in toto. It is important to understand that there is a critical difference between the government *provi-*

sion of goods and services and government *funding* of goods and services—the former is socialism, with all the ineffectiveness and misallocation of resources that entails, while the latter is the problematic but greatly preferable social welfare model. Consider the difference between social welfare as it is applied to food and socialism as it is applied to education: We have food stamps for the poor; we do not have government-owned farms, distribution networks, warehouses, and grocery stores. But we do have government-owned and government-operated schools. Voucher advocates sometimes joke that what they want are not food stamps but "school stamps," and note that the food stamp program, for all of its shortcomings, has a good track record of getting its job done for the poor while not introducing massive disruptions and distortions into the agricultural or retail grocery markets. Vouchers are a key reform not only because they allow students to attend private schools, but because they shift the locus of control in the allocation of education funds from the State acting *in loco parentis* to the consumer—or, in the case of children, to the consumers' parents acting *in loco emptori.*

This promises to bring significant benefits through disciplining and rationalizing the use of educational resources. The United States currently spends about 145 percent of the average among countries in the Organisation for Economic Co-operation and Development, of which it is a member, on education, but its results are toward the back of the OECD pack. According to Agence France-Presse, "The three-yearly OECD Programme for International Student Assessment (PISA) report, which compares the knowledge and skills of 15-year-olds in 70 countries around the world, ranked the United States 14th out of 34 OECD countries for reading skills, 17th for science, and a below-average 25th for mathematics." Total federal, state, and local spending on education in inflation-adjusted dollars per pupil is today about twice what it was in 1985, and yet results have been stagnant or worse.

While the K–12 system is a well-documented nightmare of bureaucracy and union self-dealing, even the American higher education system shows signs of radical misallocation of resources, as research from Texas education analyst Rick O'Donnell shows. As the *Texas Tribune* reports:

> In his analysis, O'Donnell divides faculty into five categories: 'dodgers,' 'coasters,' 'sherpas,' 'pioneers' and 'stars.' In this system, coasters have low teaching loads and very little externally funded research. Dodgers are the most extreme segment of coasters. Sherpas have high teaching loads and low research funding. Pioneers have the inverse of that. And stars have both high teaching loads and high levels of research funding. O'Donnell found most professors at UT and A&M to be either dodgers or coasters, which he says presents significant savings opportunities. If UT eliminated its 1,748 dodgers, who teach an average of 71 students per year at an average cost of $4,613 per student, O'Donnell calculates the 1,280 coasters—who currently teach an average of 112 students per year at an average cost of $3,044 per student—could each take on 97 more students, saving the university $573 million each year.

What would that mean, in practical terms? "That's enough to completely eliminate tuition and still have $65 million left over to refund the state taxpayer, who could use it to hire, for instance, 1,407 K–12 teachers," O'Donnell says. The figures at Texas A&M are comparable, and many state universities have even less effective allocations of teaching resources. (Note that O'Donnell's analysis takes into account both teaching loads and scholarly research.)

In short, the University of Texas could repeal tuition if only it would make more intelligent use of its labor resources. Doing so would be very popular, and, more important, it would ease the financial burden on academically talented students in Texas, which is a relatively poor state. But this will not happen, because the professorate and the higher education bureaucracy are deeply entrenched in the political class, and are more than capable of protecting their interests. O'Donnell was in fact fired by the University of Texas System for criticizing these inefficiencies. It is important to remember that not all inefficiencies are a total loss—most political inefficiencies serve somebody's interests. That certainly is true in this case. For one thing, professors do not want to be made to work harder or to give up the medieval institution of tenure and their other perquisites. For another, tuition serves a political purpose, as former University of Texas chancellor Hans Mark explains: controlling enrollment. It is politically difficult for state universities to raise their admission standards. This is particularly true of the University of Texas, which desires to practice an illegal form of race-based admissions and would have less flexibility in managing the racial makeup of its student body if there were a baseline increase in the standard for admittance, which would have a disproportionate effect on black and Latino students. Higher tuition serves to discourage enrollment without the political difficulty of raising standards, and it increases the university's cash flow—win-win, at least for the tweeds-and-tenure set.

For the rest of us, there are some real losses. Total federal, state, and local spending on education in the United States in fiscal year 2010 was $888 billion—more than is spent on national defense, welfare, or any other government function other than pensions and health care. By 2016, that number is expected to top $1.2 trillion. Achieving efficiencies on costs that large will make hundreds of billions of dollars available for more productive use, and one of those uses almost certainly will be education—but functional education. Having government spend $1.2 trillion on education does not mean that we get $1.2 trillion in value—in fact, it almost ensures that we do not. Only markets can allocate capital to its most productive use.

Applied to K–12 education, market reforms would almost certainly mean a shift away from college-preparatory education to vocational programs. Because our schools cannot tell their customers from their product, they do not in many cases provide the sort of education that students actually want—which, incidentally, is also the sort that employers say they need. As the American Enterprise Institute reports:

> Four-year colleges and universities are reluctant to see the education they provide as "occupational." High schools are often rated according to how many of their students go off to a four-year college, not how many find success in the labor market out of high school or move on to an occupational program at a community college. Overlaying all of this is an intense sensitivity to charges that disadvantaged students are being pushed onto educational pathways that do not lead to a bachelor's degree.

> But employment projections suggest that prioritizing only bachelor's-degree production is a mistake. The Georgetown Center for Education and the Workforce projects that U.S. employers will have 47 million job openings between 2010 and 2018, 30 million of which will require some post-secondary

education. Fourteen million of these positions will require an associate's degree or a vocational certificate rather than a bachelor's degree—the so-called middle-skill jobs such as electrician, health-care aide, and construction manager. Based on these projections, the Georgetown researchers estimate that by 2025, the U.S. will require 4 million additional occupational certificates and 1 million more associate's degrees to meet employer demand.

Surveys of employers routinely uncover a mismatch between what they need from their employees and what prospective hires of all educational backgrounds bring to the table. A 2006 survey of employers by the Conference Board found that 42 percent of respondents considered the overall preparation of recent high-school graduates for entry-level jobs "deficient." A similar survey by the Association of American Colleges and Universities reported that 63 percent of employers believe recent college graduates lack the skills necessary for success in the global economy.

For their part, students wish that their high-school and college courses were more closely tied to the world of work. The 2009 High School Survey of Student Engagement revealed that 40 percent of high-school students were bored in school because the curriculum was not relevant to the real world. Just 26 percent thought that high school provided skills necessary for work after graduation.

Students want it, employers need it—but the schools will not provide it.

Harvard will always be Harvard, and there will always be a need for a traditional humanities and liberal arts education for the intellectual elite. There will also be a need for such an education for those who are not among the intellectual elite but desire it and are willing to pay for it. And there are preprofessional programs in fields such as engineering and accounting that prepare students for particular occupations. But the fact is that a great many young people enrolling in four-year bachelor's degree programs are not doing so because they discern a great aching in their souls to read Plato or to study Renaissance engravings. The bachelor's degree is America's general purpose credential, our semi-official national ticket to the good life. It is not really in most cases a certification that a graduate has been thoroughly educated in a particular field of study relevant to his postgraduation career. Rather, it is a means of signaling to employers that a job candidate has a particular level of intellectual achievement, that he is capable of applying himself to both rote and challenging tasks for an extended period of time, that he can follow certain kinds of rules, and the like. But for the student who does not really desire to study an academic subject for four years, and for the employer who does not need employees who have the kind of knowledge produced by such studies, there is an enormous opportunity cost to a college education. In many such cases, both parties would be more efficiently served by administering IQ tests to job candidates and then training them to the job.

Very likely, an education market would be broadly bifurcated into a job-training sector and a liberal arts and sciences sector. For aspiring academics, lawyers, engineers, and scientists, there would be little difference between the two. For aspiring metal fabricators, the two would be strongly delineated. Academically indefensible practices such as the four-year journalism degree or the four-year business administration degree probably would disappear, being partly replaced by internships and specialized workplace training.

Competition, the increasing use of technology, and, above all, the rational allocation of resources would bring prices down.

That lattermost point is important to emphasize. The usual objection to an education market is that unless education is "free" (education is not free), poor children will not have access to it. But education already is very expensive, and the poor pay disproportionately high prices for it while receiving disproportionately poor service. Because public schools are funded largely through property taxes, it is generally assumed that nonhomeowners do not contribute to them. The poor do tend more often to rent, which means that they pay 100 percent of their landlords' property taxes (sometimes collected at a higher rate for commercial rental properties) while receiving none of the tax benefits that go along with homeownership. The economics literature suggests that such indirect taxes fall very heavily on the poor, while there is ample research documenting that public school students in poor neighborhoods have educational outcomes far inferior to those of their middle-class peers, even when the level of spending is the same. So the poor already are paying very dearly for education in many instances, and not getting much for it. And yet the poor do not seem so poor when it comes to other kinds of consumer goods. According to 2005 data, the average poor family in the United States has air-conditioning, cable TV service, two televisions, a DVD player, a washer and dryer, and one or more cars (and a third of them have two or more cars). Most of the poor have cell phones and computers. In other words, the typical poor family in the United States today enjoys goods and services that in 1950 were available only to the very wealthy, if they were available at all. Today's poverty line, $22,350 for a family of four, is in inflation-adjusted dollars about the same as the median family income in 1950. The average American house today is twice the size of the average American house in the 1950s, even though families have grown smaller. Which is not to say, "Oh, look at those pampered poor!" This simply demonstrates that we have a very good track record for making ourselves—*all* of us—richer over time, as measured by the consumption of real goods and services. There are, in fact, only a few sectors where that does not hold true: education, as we have demonstrated; general government services; and, most notable, health care.

Of course, achieving economic efficiencies is not nearly enough—nor is it a compelling end in and of itself. The question is not merely how to provide education more cheaply, but how to provide education, period, when we currently fail to do so for so many. A glimpse at how that might work can be found in one of the few authentically radical movements in America today: homeschoolers. Homeschool families have the benefit of thousands of products, from ready-made curriculum to narrowly tailored education aids, a wave of innovation unleashed by the emergence of a genuine marketplace in educational services. The etatist camp naturally regards this phenomenon with undisguised horror. Consider the words of Professor Robin West of Georgetown University's law school: "The husbands and wives in these families feel themselves to be under a religious compulsion to have large families, a homebound and submissive wife and mother who is responsible for the schooling of the children, and only one breadwinner. These families are not living in romantic, rural, self-sufficient farmhouses; they are in trailer parks, 1,000-square-foot homes, houses owned by relatives, and some, on tarps in fields or parking lots. Their lack of job skills, passed from one generation to the next, depresses the community's overall economic health and their state's tax base." As usual, the State's interest—the tax base, the "overall economic health" of the community—takes precedence over the specific needs of specific individuals and families.

West's criticism is a canard: Homeschooling families in fact have higher average incomes than nonhomeschool families, a fact that she acknowledges and then tries to magic away by invoking the "radically fundamentalist movement family," the one she locates on tarps in parking lots but in fact seems to exist largely in her head. West is forthright about the statist origins of her horror: "Parents in many states have full authority, free of all state oversight, to determine the content of their children's education," which we apparently are expected to regard with horror surpassed only by the prospect of life in a thousand-square-foot house. West writes longingly of the golden age when practically all education was conducted under the tutelage of the state and opting out of the system was forbidden— and "parents who did so were criminals." If West wanted to drive a Zaporozhets, the infamous Soviet "people's car," it would be her business, though I'll wager she drives something nicer. It would be quite another thing for her to demand that everybody drive a Zaporozhets, and that people who decline to do so be made criminals. Yet she is comfortable demanding that everybody be forced to use the Zaporozhets of education.

An effective education system is emerging, from homeschooling to high-tech distance learning to radically innovative initiatives like the privately run for-profit Acton School of Business, which offers a one-year MBA program with courses taught exclusively by actual real-world entrepreneurs, who are paid according to their student evaluations. While New York City is paying thousands of teachers not to teach, as part of its infamous "rubber room" program for nonperforming faculty, Acton dismisses its lowest-rated professor every year. Such innovations will continue to emerge, simply because education is too precious a commodity to be left to the political monopoly, a fact attested to by the real-world actions of everybody from homeschooling families to the millions of public school teachers who put their own children in private schools.

Very likely, the education system of the future will be no "system" at all, but several systems, a modular approach to education in which a combination of learning at home, in school (probably several schools, though they may share the same building), online, and throughout one's career helps us to rationally deploy our resources in order to maximize our most important one: human capital. The State could help things along by establishing vouchers, liberalizing rules for teacher credentialing and school certification, and encouraging radical experimentation rather than punishing it. But we aren't asking its permission—change is happening, whether the State likes it or not.

CHAPTER 7

Nine Hundred Kinds of Shampoo, One Law?

A shepherd, watching his Ass feeding in a meadow, was alarmed all of a sudden by the cries of the enemy. He appealed to the Ass to fly with him, lest they should both be captured, but the animal lazily replied, "Why should I, pray? Do you think it likely the conqueror will place on me two sets of panniers?" "No," rejoined the Shepherd. "Then," said the Ass, "as long as I carry the panniers, what matters it to me whom I serve?"

—AESOP'S FABLES

So the guy who invented PayPal has just reinvented military intelligence. The legendary Silicon Valley entrepreneur Peter Thiel, best known for founding the popular online payment service PayPal and for his early investments in Facebook, has a new product on the market called Palantir, after the magical seeing-stones in *The Lord of the Rings*. Palantir is a classic Silicon Valley product, designed to analyze vast databases maintained by various U.S. military, intelligence, and law enforcement agencies and ferret out nonobvious relationships and data trends. It is a piece of software inspired by the question, What would it have taken to have prevented the terrorist attacks of September 11, 2001?

Palantir can produce instant dossiers "on everything from Afghan villages to crooked bankers," as *Business Insider* puts it. "The software was developed with the idea that had it existed in 2001, 9/11 would have been obvious. Palantir would have been able to identify the pilots as people of interest from countries that harbor terrorists, connecting that with money wired around, and connecting *that* with one-way airline tickets to create actionable intelligence." Beyond the military and police agencies, Palantir has been used by JPMorgan Chase to investigate financial crimes, by investigative journalists reporting on human trafficking, and by humanitarian organizations identifying victims of the 2010 Haiti earthquake. It is no surprise that Thiel is involved in a project that is leveling the intelligence-gathering powers of the private and political sectors: He founded PayPal in part because he wanted to create a private currency free from government control. He describes his despairing view of the political enterprise to the *New Yorker*: "At its best, politics is pretty bad, and at its worst it's really ugly. So I think it would be good if we had a less political world. . . . There is always a question whether the escape from politics is somehow a selfish thing to do. You can say the whole Internet has something very escapist to it. . . . In a society where things are not great and a lot of stuff is fairly dysfunctional, that may actually be the thing where you can add the most value. You can say that's an escapist impulse of sorts, or an anti-political impulse, but maybe it is also the best way you can actually help things in this country."

We have considered some aspects of private, cooperative, nonpolitical models for doing a great deal of what government does: education, financing health care, providing for the poor. But what about law and law enforcement themselves—the fundamental architecture of politics? Here, too, what seems to be a shockingly radical assertion—that order does not come exclusively from government, and that government is not always necessary for achieving it—will turn out to have roots in very familiar places.

Since the 1970s, the Miami-based Ackerman Group (for which I did a few writing and editing assignments many years ago) has been acting as an in-house intelligence agency and, when necessary, police force for a range of top-shelf corporate clients. The firm, founded by former CIA operative Mike Ackerman, performs a number of traditional intelligence functions, from political risk analysis to advising overseas businessmen about street-level crime. They investigate potential business partners and contractors, assess the honesty and dependability of local political authorities, and advise clients about choosing secure locations for facilities and events. But the main draw of the firm is this: If you get kidnapped, they will come and get you—provided your insurance policy covers it.

The Ackerman Group is one relatively small enterprise in a very large industry dedicated to the problem of kidnapping, hostage taking, and extortion. Chubb is a global leader in the multibillion-dollar segment of the insurance industry that is now so widespread as to have its own shorthand: "K'n'R"—kidnapping and ransom. The U.S. government does not negotiate with terrorists. Your insurance company probably does. Which policy would you rather have in effect if you were kidnapped?

The Ackerman Group and similar agencies present a challenge to our traditional understanding of law enforcement. Politics, conceiving of itself as an ethical enterprise, proceeds as though law enforcement were about justice. Ackerman and other private firms do not provide justice, but a different good entirely: security. If you happen to be targeted by FARC kidnappers in Colombia or the Pakistani Taliban, the good you will undoubtedly prefer is security. Justice may be of some comfort to your family, but odds are you will not be around to appreciate it.

Administering justice through cooperative nongovernmental enterprise is a complicated proposition, though by no means beyond imagining. Providing security privately is a much simpler question—and people have been doing it for a long time.

Abilene, Kansas, was the archetypal Wild West cattle town—given that in its early history it had no formal government or police agencies, it was literally lawless. It was also remarkably safe. Abilene had about as many murders per capita during its Wild West days as it does today, sometimes fewer. The same is almost universally true of the infamous cow towns of the era. The Wild West was not so wild. I am, I admit, being a little tricky with the statistics. Abilene had a lower per capita murder rate in 1869 and 1870 than it did in 2007 because it had no murders at all in those years, while in 2007 it had one. During the most lawless of its Wild West years, it typically saw one or two murders a year. With a much smaller population today (less than seven thousand) Abilene rarely sees a murder, though it has several rapes and violent assaults per annum. The same is true for many of the other infamously lawless towns of the frontier, as Terry L. Anderson notes in his essay "The Not So Wild, Wild West."

> The taste for the dramatic in literature and other entertainment forms has led to concentration on the seeming disparity between the Westerners' desire for order and the prevailing disorder. If the Hollywood image of the West were not enough to taint our view, scholars of violence have contributed with quotes such as the following: "We can report with some assurance that compared to frontier days there has been a significant decrease in crimes of violence in the United States."

Recently, however, more careful examinations of the conditions that existed cause one to doubt the accuracy of this perception. In his book, *Frontier Violence: Another Look*, W. Eugene Hollon stated that he believed "that the Western frontier was a far more civilized, more peaceful, and safer place than American society is today." The legend of the "wild, wild West" lives on despite Robert Dykstra's finding that in five of the major cattle towns (Abilene, Ellsworth, Wichita, Dodge City, and Caldwell) for the years from 1870 to 1885, only 45 homicides were reported—an average of 1.5 per cattle-trading season.

. . . Only two towns, Ellsworth in 1873 and Dodge City in 1876, ever had 5 killings in any one year. Frank Prassel states in his book subtitled *A Legacy of Law and Order*, that "if any conclusion can be drawn from recent crime statistics, it must be that this last frontier left no significant heritage of offenses against the person, relative to other sections of the country."

Like Abilene, Dodge City's murder rate today is not much different from what it was during the Wild West era: between one and three most years. Wichita today has many *more* murders than it did without formal law enforcement, sometimes running as high as forty or more in a single year. If the historical evidence is to be believed, cattle drives through the lawless Wild West boomtowns were considerably safer than, for example, the streets of a typical large U.S. city with a multibillion-dollar police department on the evening of a major sports championship, or about as dangerous as spending spring break at Padre Island, Texas (and a good deal less dangerous than spending spring break in Acapulco).

How did they keep the peace?

Ronald Coase, a Nobel laureate in economics, considered that problem in his article "The Problem of Social Cost," which has the distinction of being the most-cited law review article in all of academic literature. Coase argued that laws, like any other product, can only be justified by taking into account cost-benefit analysis, and that in many legal disputes conflicts that are taken to be the "fault" of a single party are in fact merely cases of unaligned interests between the parties. In most cases, he maintained, the disputant parties should be able to negotiate an efficient settlement except for the presence of "transaction costs"—the expense and hassle involved in gathering information, engaging in negotiations, executing a settlement, and the like. In a world of zero transaction costs—a very theoretical world indeed—no legal rules would be necessary: People would simply bargain with one another to produce the most efficient distribution of resources regardless of abstract notions of rights and legal requirements.

One of Coase's thought experiments involved theoretical disputes between farmers and ranchers—he was born in 1910, and such disputes were part of the intellectual weather of his time. Historically, there have indeed been persistent tensions between those two occupations, usually revolving around the fact that ranch animals often stray onto farmland and do damage to crops and other properties. Some decades later, the Yale legal scholar Robert Ellickson had the wit to put Coase's theoretical exercise to a real-world test, examining dispute resolution practices between farmers and ranchers in Shasta County, California. What he discovered was fascinating: Not only do neighbors in Shasta County solve their property disputes without availing themselves of formal legal institutions, but most of them do not even know what the law says about their particular cases—and the local legal authorities were the ones with the least knowledge about the letter of the law. Writes Ellickson: "People frequently resolve their disputes in cooperative fashion without paying any attention to the laws that apply to those disputes. This thesis has broad implications for how political debates should be conducted, how lawyers should practice their profession, and how law schools and social-science departments should educate their students. I did not appreciate how unimportant law can be when I embarked on this project." As with the mutual aid insurance programs described above, these processes are driven by cooperation, mutual interest, trust, reputation, and the necessity of making repeated transactions with the same parties over long periods of time and touching many subjects.

What Ellickson discovered is that Coase had in fact been too cautious in his estimate of how little people require recourse to the formal law, even when transaction costs are not zero. He writes:

If Shasta County residents were to act like the farmer and the rancher in Coase's parable, they would settle their trespass problems in the following way. First, they would look to the formal law to determine who had what entitlements. They would regard those substantive rules as beyond their influence (as "exogenous," to use the economists' adjective). When they faced a potentially costly interaction, such as a trespass risk to crops, they would resolve it "in the shadow of" the formal legal rules.

... In rural Shasta County, where transaction costs are assuredly not zero, trespass conflicts are generally resolved not in "the shadow of the law" but, rather, beyond that shadow. Most rural residents are consciously committed to an overarching norm of cooperation among neighbors.

The residents of Shasta County exhibit two bedrock American virtues: a live-and-let-live philosophy and a deep distaste for lawyers. The prevailing social norms hold that even if one's legal rights have been violated, calling in lawyers represents a kind of moral failure on the part of the complainant. This is even true when dealing with what Ellickson calls the "deviants"—the small number of residents who do not care about their reputations and do not hold to the norm of neighborly cooperation. Ellickson's report here is worth quoting at some length:

> When milder measures such as gossip fail, a person is regarded as being justified in threatening to use, and perhaps even actually using, tougher self-help sanctions. Particularly in unfenced country, a victim may respond to repeated cattle trespasses by herding the offending animals to a location extremely inconvenient for their owner. Another common response to repeated trespasses is to threaten to kill a responsible animal should it ever enter again. Although the killing of trespassing livestock is a crime in California, six landowners—not noticeably less civilized than the others—unhesitatingly volunteered that they had issued death threats of this sort. These threats are credible in Shasta County because victims of recurring trespasses, particularly if they have first issued a warning, feel justified in killing or injuring the mischievous animals.
>
> Despite the criminality of the conduct (a fact not necessarily known to the respondents), I learned the identity of two persons who had shot trespassing cattle. Another landowner told of running the steer of an uncooperative neighbor into a fence. The most intriguing report came from a rancher who

had had recurrent problems with a trespassing bull many years before. This rancher told a key law enforcement official that he wanted to castrate the bull—"to turn it into a steer." The official replied that he would turn a deaf ear if that were to occur. The rancher asserted that he then carried out his threat.

It is difficult to estimate how frequently rural residents actually resort to violent self-help. Nevertheless, fear of physical retaliation is undoubtedly one of the major incentives for order in rural Shasta County. Ranchers who run herds at large freely admit that they worry that their trespassing cattle might meet with violence. One traditionalist reported that he is responsive to complaints from ranchette owners because he fears they will poison or shoot his stock. A judge for a rural district of the county asserted that a vicious animal is likely to "disappear" if its owner does not control it. A resident of the Oak Run area stated that some area residents responded to [noted deviant] Frank Ellis' practice of running herds at large by rustling Ellis' cattle. He suggested that Ellis print tee shirts with the inscription: "Eat Ellis Beef. Everyone in Oak Run Does!"

Notice that not only are the residents of Shasta County able to resolve their disputes without recourse to the law; they also violate the formal law in doing so—with the encouragement of the local legal authorities. This system works quite well for them. Farmers expect some minor damage to their fences and forage in the natural course of things, both from stray cattle and from wildlife, especially deer. And most of them expect that over time they will be on both sides of trespass disputes: Even the nonranching farmers often keep some small amount of livestock, or at least dogs, which sometimes harm smaller animals or do other damage. Their usual response to a stray animal is to simply call its owner, who regards the call as a favor rather than as a complaint. The owners often offer to pay restitution for damage caused, but Ellickson could find almost nobody who had ever accepted such payment except in cases of repeated trespass and negligence.

Just as in the case of our mutual aid insurance societies, voluntary associations and cooperative practices show a remarkable ability to align the individual interest (protecting one's property) with our social interest (resolving conflicts in a nondisruptive fashion that maximizes the efficient allocation of material resources).

Property disputes are one thing—what about more serious crimes? As Anderson found in the case of the not-so-wild West, residents in areas without formal government law enforcement mechanisms proved similarly adept at creating private enforcement agencies, ad hoc courts, and other methods for settling disputes. Mining camps, land clubs, cattlemen's associations, and wagon trains all developed their own models of law and law enforcement. Sanctions ranged from exile in the case of wagon trains to the hiring of private marshals and capital punishment in the case of serious crimes. Many of these arrangements were ad hoc, of course, but that is not necessarily a criticism: Formal law enforcement institutions make mistakes (and worse) without being able to adapt quickly to new conditions. Anderson reached three major conclusions:

1. The West, although often dependent upon market peacekeeping agencies, was, for the most part, orderly.
2. Different standards of justice did prevail and various preferences for rules were expressed through the market place.

3. Competition in defending and adjudicating rights does
   have beneficial effects. Market agencies provided useful ways of measuring the efficiency of government
   alternatives. The fact that government's monopoly on
   coercion was not taken as seriously as at present meant
   that when that monopoly was poorly used, market alternatives arose. Even when these market alternatives
   did become "governments" in the sense of having a
   virtual monopoly on coercion, the fact that such firms
   were usually quite small provided significant checks on
   their behavior. Clients could leave or originate protective agencies on their own. Without formal legal sanctions, the private agencies did face a "market test" and
   the rate of survival of such agencies was much less than
   under government.

In the early twenty-first century, the United States already is full
of private courts enforcing private law. In Silicon Valley, it is a tru-
ism that disputes over issues such as patents and complex contracts
may be honest disagreements or malicious advantage seeking. The
honest cases go to arbitration, and the malicious cases go to court—
meaning political courts.

One highly regarded private court is the Silicon Valley Arbitration Center. It probably would not describe itself as a private court,
but that is in fact what it is. It describes its business as resolving
"disputes involving contracts, sales, licensing, distribution, services, marketing, patents, copyrights, trademarks, trade secrets,
joint ventures, strategic relationships, partnerships, corporations,
corporate securities, company management, corporate governance,
stockholders, equity investment, debt financing, mergers, acquisi-

tions, dissolutions and other corporate, commercial and intellectual property matters. In addition to resolving U.S. based disputes, SVAC provides resolution of international disputes involving parties in the Americas, Europe, the Middle East, Africa and Asia."

Such agencies exist for many reasons. The courts are slow and inefficient, and they are—we are not supposed to notice—subject to political pressure. And Silicon Valley is very much haunted by the spirit of Thomas Penfield Jackson, the presiding judge in the 1990s Microsoft antitrust case. Microsoft had its defenders and its trenchant critics (though how you argue that a firm is employing monopoly tactics when it doesn't even have 20 percent market share is beyond me), but the tech-heads and alpha geeks on both sides of the battle were embarrassed and horrified that a case involving technical questions about the development and distribution of software and services was being presided over by a judge who had never so much as used a computer or operated a mouse, and who had to have the most elementary technical terms explained to him. People involved in good-faith disputes want their cases handled by analysts with high levels of issue-specific expertise. Patent trolls and tort vultures pray for Thomas Penfield Jackson.

The extent to which such private law and enforcement agencies can replace traditional political law is of course unknown. The anarchist theorist David Friedman (son of the aforementioned Milton Friedman) has drawn up elaborate theoretical models of such a society, spelled out in his provocative book, *The Machinery of Freedom*. Friedman gives a great deal of thought to how particular private law agencies are likely to shape up and foresees a situation in which competing private police/protection agencies develop bilateral agreements about which third-party private courts to use in the case of disputes between protective agencies. Legal codes and police agencies would compete on the marketplace like brands of diet cola. It is a rollicking read, but I think Friedman errs in having excessive confidence in his own powers of prediction. It is in the nature of all complex systems—including all markets—to evolve in unexpected ways. The question we should be asking ourselves is not "What does a good cooperative law enforcement system look like?" but "In what sort of environment might better law enforcement practices evolve?" We probably would be better off on net as a society if, for example, the hotly contested question of the legal definition of marriage were left to the evolutionary process of private contracts and social experimentation. Labor law might look like an example of grossly unfair competition in the marketplace—how much power does a job seeker really have against the behemoth corporation deciding whether to hire him?—which again points to the necessity of developing peer-to-peer mutual aid societies to help level the playing field.

Let me conclude here with another thought experiment: We recoil from the prospect of putting a price on human life, but both insurance companies and courts do that every day in the course of pursuing their business. Let us imagine a court that is truly open to arbitration, and install me there as the recently convicted defendant in a homicide case. The average time served for a homicide is, as noted earlier, 5.5 years. But let us imagine that I am a very rich man and terrified of prison. I might offer the family of the victim $1 million if they will agree to cut my sentence down to two years, and $10 million if they agree that I will do no jail time at all. Would it be unseemly to do so? Would it fail to serve justice? Many people would answer "Yes," that the rich should not be able to buy their way out of a prison term for homicide.

Let's put a slight spin on the case: Maybe the murder victim was not the pleasant honors student who always seems to be the victim in high-profile murder cases. Let's say he was a twice-convicted felon and gang member—much more typical of the profile of a murder victim in the United States in the early twenty-first century. Would that complicate things? What if his family were very poor, and he left behind a severely disabled child whose life would be radically improved by my paying $10 million to his family, even if that means I never see the inside of a prison. Would that be unjust?

Our system of justice is based largely on retribution—and in many cases retribution seems appropriate. The desire for vengeance is not always antisocial. But I suspect that if we were able to negotiate more among ourselves, in most cases we would develop practices that are based less on retribution and more on restitution. Just as security before the fact is preferable to justice after the fact, restitution in many if not most cases is preferable to retribution. A murder or a rape cannot be undone by a $10 million payment—but it won't be undone by locking somebody away in a prison cell for 5.5 years, either. Perhaps you find that distasteful—but do you think that you have the right to make that decision on behalf of a family whose values may differ from your own, whose interests are only incidental to your own, and about whom you know either next to nothing or literally nothing? Even in the most heinous cases, one-size-fits-all law is not necessarily justice.

As always, we have to consider the real-world alternative. A few years back, there was an amusing if dismaying episode in which Congress attempted to do something good. For years, there had persisted a glaring discrepancy in how drug dealers and users were punished for crack cocaine versus conventional powder cocaine—in fact, the disparity in prison sentence length was one hundred to one by weight. It was widely noted that crack use tended to be concentrated among the poor and the black, while powder cocaine was favored by the wealthy and the white, and that the poor and the black were being punished one hundred times more harshly for essentially the same offense. The injustice of it was enough that even Congress was finally moved to act. But there was a problem—neither party wanted to be thought of as the soft-on-crack party, and the legislation was held up because members of both parties were afraid that they would get credit for an important legal reform nobody wanted credit for. House leaders finally arranged for the bill to be passed on unanimous consent, meaning that there would be no roll call vote and no record. An important piece of legislation was passed—but only on the condition that nobody would know who was responsible for doing the right thing. Today crack possession is punished "only" eighteen times more harshly than possession of powder cocaine. Private law will have disadvantages, but so does political law.

Political law is problematic because it does not deliver on its promises. The theory of the rule of law holds that the law is prospective (you can reliably know ahead of time what the law says and thereby avoid breaking it), consistent, and applied without regard to the socioeconomic standing or political influence of the plaintiff and defendant. Political law satisfies none of those conditions.

At the simplest theoretical level, the myth of the rule of law seems plausible enough. If the speed limit is 55 miles an hour, you cannot be given a speeding ticket for driving 45 miles an hour. If you are caught driving 65 miles an hour, you will be convicted of speeding and you will face a fine or some other form of punishment that has been determined in advance and written into the statute. Our ability to know the rules and to know the consequences of breaking them, together with the knowledge that the rules are applied the same way to all of us—that the law is "no respecter of persons"—is what commands our allegiance to the rule of law.

And it is the actual experience of getting a speeding ticket that undermines it. As it turns out, in many jurisdictions you *can* get a speeding ticket for driving 45 miles per hour in a 55-mile-per-hour zone, if conditions are such that a police officer believes 45 miles per hour to be an unsafe speed. The converse experience of police discretion—the fact that few police officers will write you a ticket for driving three miles per hour over the speed limit—is much more common. There is a great deal of official discretion built into every level of the system, from the police on the scene to the prosecutor considering charges to the judge hearing the case. And the authorities are respecters of persons—you don't meet a lot of police officers, prosecutors, or judges who pay a lot of speeding tickets.

But discretion in law enforcement is hardly an insurmountable problem. In fact, it is not *necessarily* a problem; a system with no discretion at all probably would prove inhumane. But that discretion interacts with an inconvenient fact that rarely enters into democratic discourse: The law itself is a mishmash of incompatible rules and contradictory precedents. The proposition at the heart of our idea of the rule of law—that there is a correct answer to any given legal question, independent of the politics and preferences of the people empowered to make legal decisions—is a myth. In our political imagination, a legal dispute is akin to a logic problem: There are premises and rules, and from them we can deduct conclusions. In truth, the structure of legal reasoning is less like classical logic and more like scriptural debate. Because the law contains contradictory rules and precedents, a valid chain of legal reasoning can be created to accommodate almost any desired outcome in any given case.

When it comes to disputes under the law, Oliver Wendell Holmes Jr. practiced law without romance: "You can give *any* conclusion a logical form."

Over time, the consequences of such willy-nilly jurisprudence begin to accrete in an unsightly way. The law does not resemble a structure, but a sediment. To take the most obvious example, there is no plausible legal explanation for the fact that constitutional rights of the most robust kind—the ones that actually are written into the Constitution—by and large enjoy less judicial protection than do the constitutional rights that judges have imagined into the founding document. Whatever your opinion about gun rights or abortion, it is undeniable that one of those subjects is contemplated in the Bill of Rights, and given formal protection, while the other one makes no appearance. Perhaps you believe that the Second Amendment should be interpreted narrowly. Perhaps you believe that abortion ought to be entirely unrestricted. Those are perfectly valid beliefs, but there is nothing in the content of the language of the Constitution that can in good faith be read to provide simultaneously for the limitation of plainly stated constitutional rights and the expansion of nonconstitutional rights. Constitutional jurisprudence is thick with these paradoxes. The First Amendment was written with the intent of protecting political speech, but under our current regime political speech rights enjoy less robust First Amendment protections than do the gyrations of strippers at New Jersey topless joints or magazines specializing in the depiction of exotic sex acts. Sodomy is a constitutional right; criticizing Mitt Romney on the radio during the run-up to an election is not. There clearly is something out of balance here.

This is not merely a question of liberal judicial activism. Andrew C. McCarthy, a former federal prosecutor, has argued that the federal statute outlawing torture does not outlaw torture, so long as that torture is used to extract information from our prisoners: "As a matter of law," he writes, "CIA waterboarding—like the same waterboarding actions featured in Navy SEALs training—cannot be torture because there is no intention to inflict severe mental or physical pain; the exercise is done for a different purpose," that purpose being to gain useful intelligence on terrorists' activities. As a pure matter of legal reasoning, I have no doubt that McCarthy is correct. But if he is correct, then the only torture that is illegal is torture that is performed to no end. That is to say, if this legal reasoning is correct, the law purporting to outlaw torture is in fact a law that legalizes torture. And if the statute does outlaw torture, McCarthy stands ready to argue that the separation of powers in the Constitution means that the president need not follow "mere congressional statute"—what you and I might call "the law"—so long as he invokes national security while doing so. Torture is not torture, the law is not the law. Alice falls deeper down the rabbit hole.

Professor John Hasnas of Georgetown goes a step further in his essay "The Myth of the Rule of Law," arguing that "it is impossible to reach an objective decision based solely on the law. This is because the law is always open to interpretation and *there is no such thing as a normatively neutral interpretation* (emphasis in original)." The law, examined critically, is inherently political. It offers no respite from the arbitrary exercise of state power by self-interested state actors. Hasnas points to the Fourteenth Amendment's equal-protection clause: Within living memory, the American judicial establishment interpreted that language as being perfectly consistent with the "separate but equal" arrangements of the segregation era. Later, it was interpreted to mean that the government could make few, if any, racial distinctions among its citizens. Still later, it was interpreted to mean that the government could make racial distinctions among its citizens for "benign" purposes, meaning reparative discrimination for blacks and, secondarily, for other legally protected groups. Some interpretations now hold that the law requires such reparative discrimination. So the equal-protection clause today means precisely the opposite of what it did a generation or two ago. The law did not change. The judges changed.

This jerky evolution has the unhappy effect of making it impossible, in some circumstances, to comply with the law—and as we move beyond such relatively trivial issues as speeding tickets and on to major political questions, the complexities and contradictions are dramatic. In the *Ricci v. DeStefano* case, the New Haven, Connecticut, fire department found itself in an impossible legal position: Because black applicants did relatively poorly on the department's exam, using the test results in promotion decisions would have a "disparate impact" on black firefighters, which is illegal under Title VII of the Civil Rights Act. But if it threw out the results of the exam, it would be engaging in "disparate treatment," changing its practices because of racial considerations—which is *also* illegal under Title VII of the Civil Rights Act. Either way, the city was sure to be sued. Perversely, the Supreme Court snippily decreed that trying to comply with the law is no defense against a body of law with which it is impossible to comply: "Fear of litigation alone cannot justify an employer's reliance on race to the detriment of individuals," the Court wrote. Any surprise that this was another 5–4 vote? (Any surprise that the federal judge the Supreme Court overturned in the *Ricci* case, Sonia Sotomayor, is now on the Supreme Court? Meaning that if *Ricci* were to be decided today instead of just a few years ago, the law almost certainly would be held to mean the opposite of what the law is held to mean under the current decision? Try gaming that out and discovering how to follow the law. Hint: Hire the right lawyers.)

But while the courts may lob the occasional *Ricci* or *Roe v. Wade* or *Lawrence v. Texas* legal hand grenade onto the political battle-field, American law is not radically indeterminate. In the normal course of affairs, what changes come come slowly. Our legal system, though finally arbitrary, is reasonably predictable, which is one of the things that makes the rule-of-law regime, clay-footed as it is, reasonably attractive to most Americans (who cannot, in any case, imagine an alternative to it). The naïve belief that present-day American governance represents a continuous tradition dating back to the establishment of the Constitution commands our loyalty, though it is impossible for a serious-minded person to believe that the constitutional office occupied by Barack Obama is substantially identical to the one occupied by George Washington.

If the law is arbitrary, why is it apparently so consistent? Hasnas's answer is that it is not the law that is remarkably consistent, but the lawyers: Bar and bench are staffed by strivers who were, until quite recently, overwhelmingly homogeneous in their background, ethnicity, religion, education, class, and politics. He writes:

> Typically, they are people from a solid middle- to upper-class background who performed well at an appropriately prestigious undergraduate institution; demonstrated the ability to engage in the type of analytical reasoning that is measured by the standardized Law School Admissions Test; passed through the crucible of law school, complete with its methodological and political indoctrination; and went on to high-profile careers as attorneys, probably with a prestigious Wall Street–style law firm. To have been appointed to the bench, it

is virtually certain that they were both politically moderate and well-connected. . . . It can hardly be surprising that there will be a high degree of agreement among judges as to how cases ought to be decided. But this agreement is due to the common set of normative presuppositions the judges share, not some immanent, objective meaning that exists within the rules of law.

The American legal establishment poses as a neutral interpreter of rules with fixed and objective meaning, but it is in fact simply the refiner and enforcer of ruling-class opinion and taste. In that, it has an analogue in a government that seems very different from our own but operates on very similar mechanics: Iran's Guardian Council functions as that country's supreme court, drawing from constitutional and sharia sources to oversee the whole of Iranian politics, setting aside parliamentary decisions or other acts of government as it sees fit, and ensuring that its own interpretation of Islamic law dominates all public life. That Iran's Guardian Council is nakedly political and ideological, a cold-eyed creature of political calculation, is obvious to any outside observer who does not sympathize with Tehran's peculiar religious and political enthusiasms. It strikes the liberal Westerner as the sort of thing that must be considered illegitimate, impermissible in a liberal and democratic society. Never mind that our justices perform the same function, in the same way, wearing quite similar robes.

A level of arbitrariness is tolerable in a state that is small and limited—and modest in its ambitions. The danger of that arbitrariness increases exponentially as the size and scope of the state grows. Pluck a cautionary tale from any headline. Consider orchid enthusiast George Norris of Spring, Texas, who at age sixty-five was bankrupted and then pitched into prison, possibly for the remainder of his days, because he neglected to file the right paperwork on a flower that he mailed to a federal agent, who was posing as a fellow orchid enthusiast as part of a sting operation. The absurdity of the situation is beyond the imagination of Thomas Pynchon. A state that has undercover agents posing as orchid enthusiasts is a dangerous state. Norris, the *Economist* reports, was described by prosecutors as the "kingpin" of a flower-smuggling operation; he never netted more than $20,000 in a year from his part-time floral hobby. So crowded are our prisons that Norris has two roommates—in *solitary confinement.*

The state grows, and it grows hungry. And when its legitimacy is questioned, it grows vicious. What stands between American citizens and this battered Leviathan? A convenient fiction about the "rule of law"? A fleeting hope that Sonia Sotomayor switched to decaf this morning, or that she decocted a message from Alexis de Tocqueville in the steam rising from her morning oatmeal?

The idea of having many competing legal codes instead of single sacrosanct Law sounds radical at first, until you consider that you've been living that way your entire life. Americans and Canadians live under very different bodies of law—and no body of law at all governing their relationships with each other across borders—and yet we do business with one another, travel easily back and forth between one another's countries, marry each other, build businesses together, all without an all-encompassing Law. Canadians have Canadian law, and Americans have American law. If a Canadian is murdered by an American, Canadian institutions have only such authority as has been granted them under American law; if the property of a U.S. firm is seized by the Canadian government, U.S. institutions have only such recourse as is allowed to them under Canadian law—and they never even got to vote on that. And the Canadian visiting the United States doesn't have only federal law to contend with, but that of fifty states and many more municipalities, each with its own body of laws, sometimes radically different from those of the state or the city next door. If Americans and Canadians can coexist without being equally bound by a single Law, and if Americans in Connecticut and New York State can coexist without a single overarching Law, and if New Yorkers in Woodstock can coexist with New Yorkers in Tribeca without a single Law, why should we believe that two people living in Tribeca need a single Law to settle all disputes?

If those two Tribeca residents happen to work a dozen blocks downtown on Wall Street, this already will be familiar to them. Complex international financial contracts may involve many legal jurisdictions, and counterparties generally agree in advance under which law disputes will be settled: The bestselling brands in that market are London law and New York law. Really good law and really good legal institutions are enormously valuable products—gold cannot compare. London and New York are wildly rich cities because they are the world's financial capitals, and they are the world's financial capitals in no small part because they have excellent law and honest, transparent legal institutions. Bombay is full of brilliant people, and the would-be financiers of São Paulo are no less enterprising than their British and American comrades, but São Paulo does not have London law, and Bombay does not have the most trustworthy institutions.

Both British and U.S. law ultimately derive from the English common law, which was written by . . . nobody. Unlike the Code of Hammurabi or the Ten Commandments, the most successful, most practical, most cherished legal system in the world did not have an author. Nobody planned it; no sublime legal genius thought it up. It emerged in an iterative, evolutionary manner, much like a language emerges. (Somebody invented Esperanto, which nobody uses; nobody invented English or Chinese.) English commercial and maritime law have their roots in rules developed by traders, merchants, and shippers to settle disputes among them. The key thing to appreciate is that our more useful legal codes were not the product of government, but the product of active cooperation to advance mutual economic and personal interests. The really good law precedes politics: Political law looks like Sarbanes-Oxley, the PPACA, No Child Left Behind, the PATRIOT Act, Frank-Dodd, and whatever recent turn-of-the-century nightmare you want to choose. Commercial practices reinforced the common law, and the advent of insurance, commercial banking, and other modern financial practices helped to ensure that rules became norms that were consistently adopted across firms and industries. Just as U.S. and British investment banks typically insist that financial contracts in European Union countries (especially economically distressed EU countries) include London law provisions or New York law provisions, so did the old Lloyd's of London insist that the firms with which it transacted business agree to settle disputes under what eventually evolved into the Anglo-American legal ecosystem, which has its origins in the wondrously complex and occasionally beautiful common law, the repository of many generations' worth of wisdom, careful analysis, and experimentation. Trying to replace the common law with a rationally designed regime of political law is like trying to design a better rhinoceros in a laboratory, and every step away from the common law has been a step toward legal sclerosis and distortion.

As the English commercial and maritime law demonstrate, private actors operating cooperatively in markets are more than capable of generating law—they are in fact more capable of generating useful law than legislators typically are. Law is a product like any other product: Competition makes it better and ensures that it serves the interests of consumers rather than those of producers. (Does anybody doubt that political law is a product designed to serve its producers?)

We all have experience with competing bodies of law. Texas has low taxes and a light regulatory environment, and businesses to which that is important locate operations there rather than in New York or California. Massachusetts recognizes same-sex marriages, providing gay couples from Utah with an incentive to bring their assets and their productivity to the Bay State. Medical marijuana is legal in California and a serious crime elsewhere. You cannot pick up a hooker in Florida just because prostitution is legal in Reno.

I sometimes carry a handgun. I have a license to do so in one state, which license is also recognized by some other states, though not all of them. My license is not recognized by the state of New York, but even if it were, New York City would not recognize it— and indeed it does not even recognize concealed-carry permits issued by New York State authorities. There is, of course, an app for that, which cross-references your GPS location against a database of concealed-carry laws and a list of your permits in order to let you know whether you are legal—and, more important, whether you'll be legal when you arrive at your next location. Most politicians have little interest and functionally no knowledge of legal arrangements in distant jurisdictions, except at the most superficial level. Your iPhone can tell you everything you need to know about the validity of your concealed-carry permit, yet another case of the curious Jetsons-versus-Flintstones dynamic of life lived in part under markets and in part under politics.

Privately generated law may sound exotic, but if you live in the

United States there is a 100 percent probability that you live under several privately generated statutes, for instance the Uniform Commercial Code, which was developed by the Uniform Law Commission, a committee organized by the American Bar Association in the late nineteenth century. Because states are rightly suspicious of the interference of a federal government that consistently seeks to erode or subsume their sovereignties at every turn, they began to develop model laws to harmonize differences across the states in order to head off federal intervention, and they turned to the ULC, a private agency, to do so.

Lately, the ULC has found its services in demand among U.S. Indian tribes, who find themselves in need of modern legal infrastructures in order to facilitate economic development. (Why? Because, as one Indian leader put it, "Poverty is not part of our cultural heritage.") Because the tribes have neither conventional bodies of commercial law nor in many cases credible judicial systems to enforce contracts, they have found themselves shut out of the commercial credit markets and thereby deprived of a key tool of economic development. Of particular interest are "secured transaction" laws, meaning loans or sales secured by collateral in the form of financial assets, equipment and machinery, oil and gas production, or contractual claims against future revenue streams from business operations. For example, a tribe with large natural-gas deposits might seek to use future gas revenues as collateral to take out a loan to finance development of those gas fields. Similarly, a tribal organization with valuable equipment used in one line of business might seek to use it as collateral when buying new equipment for another line of business on credit, a collateralized purchase instead of a collateralized loan. Secured-transaction law in the United States is handled under state legal codes, and state law does not apply to Indian tribes, relations with which are handled under federal law. Without a familiar legal environment, commercial lenders either will refuse to lend or will demand substantially higher interest rates and other kinds of security before making a loan, just as John Deere or Caterpillar is going to think twice about selling $1 million worth of equipment on credit if the firm is not confident that its rights will be respected in the event of a dispute or a default. Modern financial law is extremely complex, but there are prevailing norms that lenders expect to be honored, and the Indian tribal governments simply do not have the competence to develop legal satisfactory commercial legal codes, which is why some of them have turned to ULC. Both U.S. states and Indian tribes have long experimented with privately generated commercial law, with a good deal of success: Some of the ULC's provisions have been adopted by all fifty states, the District of Columbia, Puerto Rico, and the U.S. Virgin Islands.

But as Roy Cohen observed, while it matters what the law is, it may matter more who the judge is. The lack of a familiar legal code prevented investment in Indian economic development projects, but so did the lack of a credible judicial system. Indian courts developed a reputation for refusing to hand over collateral during disputes and refusing to enforce long-term contracts when the interests of tribal insiders conflicted with those of outsiders. ULC has worked to address that as well, offering judicial training workshops for those tribes adopting its statutes. More than anything else, the adoption of commercial laws that abide by modern norms is a way for tribes to signal to lenders and investors that they are ready to enter into the social network that is the contemporary global marketplace—not diminishing their sovereignty, but affirming it.

Legal systems are in many ways like languages: They are social networks that people enter into in order to expand their options and secure their interests. The English language has spread throughout the world (it is one of two official national languages in India) not because of unadulterated admiration for Anglo-American culture but because Chinese-speaking, German-speaking, and Hindi-speaking people wish to participate in the global economy, and speaking English makes that a great deal easier. There are some people in Iceland (population about 200,000) who resent that practically all Icelandic people speak at least one foreign language, usually English, and argue that the inroads made by English into Iceland represent a form of cultural colonialism. But speaking English is a way for Icelandic people to project their influence out into the broader world as much as it is a way for the Anglophone world to project its influence into Iceland. People who spoke only Icelandic would have very few people to speak to—the entire country has fewer people than Lubbock County, Texas. Likewise, an Indian tribe that insists on abjuring outside assistance in the development of its legal code at the price of cutting itself off from financial markets is unnecessarily impoverishing itself.

There is of course a world of difference between an Indian tribe deciding to seek outside help from a private agency in order to improve its legal code and an outside entity imposing its legal code on a sovereign Indian tribe. Private agencies have no such power to impose their will on anybody: They can offer their ideas, advocate them, persuade decision makers, cajole them, rebut critics, and argue ad nauseam—but they cannot force their will on anybody. Only states can do that.

This is an excellent argument for maximizing private lawmaking and minimizing political lawmaking. Take, for example, the disputatious issue of same-sex marriage. Each side claims the support of an inviolable moral principle: that homosexual couples are in the name of fairness entitled to equal treatment under the law, or that marriage is a sacred institution that preexists the state and is therefore not subject to political redefinition. The dispute often is painted as merely religious—"merely"—but sophisticated nonsectarian arguments for traditional marriage have been advanced by Professor Robert P. George of Princeton, among others, while constitutional scholars take both sides of the issue as self-evidently correct—as constitutional scholars are in the habit of doing. There is an obvious private-law alternative to the political model of marriage: the contract. Indeed, marriage was long understood as a contract, both in the Western world and beyond. The English language still contains such phrases as "the marriage contract" or "contracting a marriage with" and the like. Marriage has a sacramental and social side, of course, but there is scant reason to believe that political involvement in that aspect of marriage is called for—that churches have absolute autonomy in deciding what sort of couplings they will choose to recognize is a long-standing tradition in the Anglo-American world. What is at issue in the debate is partly symbolism but mostly the question of the marriage contract as contract.

A private model of marriage would enable many kinds of outcomes. For those to whom marriage is a purely secular question of combining assets into a single household, establishing legal relationships for the purposes of jointly sharing property and credit, enabling inheritances, etc., the privately negotiated contract is of course an ideal solution, and not without precedent. We already have prenuptial contracts, and under a private model of marriage the prenuptial contract would simply in effect become the nuptial contract. There is very little reason for anybody's objecting to agreements among third parties to share property and pool assets, regardless of whether there is a sexual component to the relationship.

If two men who are romantically involved desire to form a legal union to enable them to share financial resources, there is no more reason for the pope to object to that than if they wanted to form a corporation or a limited-liability partnership, which achieves the same thing without the sex. Many of the objections offered against same-sex marriage—that it would open the door to polygamy, for instance—are obviated by the property model of marriage, inasmuch as there is no reason to object to three people sharing their property, either, or a dozen. We may think it immoral or unseemly that three people form a single household and carry on a joint sexual relationship, but we already live in a society in which people have casual or regular sexual relationships with two or more people at the same time, and there is no move afoot to criminalize casual dating—it is difficult to imagine such a thing coming to pass. In any case, the private, contractual model of marriage allows us to separate the material question of asset sharing from the moral question of sexual relations.

For many people, marriage has a moral, social, and religious quality as well, and here again a purely contract-oriented model efficiently achieves the best balance of interests. Perhaps I am engaged to a young woman and desire to marry her. She is a Roman Catholic, and would prefer a Roman Catholic wedding. She is vociferous in this preference, to the extent of suggesting that if I do not agree to a Roman Catholic wedding then my love life is likely to come to resemble that of a Roman Catholic priest. But the Catholic Church will only officiate over weddings based on contracts that meet Catholic standards: no unresolved prior marriages, good standing in the church, proper marital preparation, etc. The Catholic Church believes that valid marriages are insoluble, meaning that if I should enter into a Catholic marriage, then I cannot divorce my wife and would remain bound to the terms of the contract—including its financial terms—unless the church should see fit to declare the marriage invalid and grant an annulment. I myself might prefer a more Woodstock model of marriage—anything goes, no-questions-asked divorce if things should come to that. But what will transpire is a three-way negotiation between myself, my betrothed, and the Catholic Church: a ménage-à-trois in the literal sense of the term.

Moral traditionalists argue that the arrangements they favor produce stronger and more functional families, and there is some evidence that they are correct. The conservative coalition in the United States includes both moral traditionalists and free-marketers, and it is curious that conservatives who believe that they do not need the government to tell them what to buy believe that they need the government to tell them whom to marry, or at least what the acceptable bounds of marriage are. This is not a merely rhetorical point. If moral traditionalists are correct that the institutions they favor will produce superior outcomes, then they should be able to compete in the social marketplace with all of those inferior products, all those off-brand marriages. Social evolution works in no small part through relatively low-status members of groups imitating relatively high-status members. Mitt Romney and his wife have by all accounts a very traditional marriage and family: a mother and a father, five sons, and, as of this writing, eighteen grandchildren. The Romneys are remarkably successful people—contrary to the political cartoons, Romney gave away his small inheritance and made his hundreds of millions of dollars on his own, and his sons also are very successful men. Most of us understand that family and childhood conditions play an important role in our lives, though not dispositive ones, and comparing the family outcomes the Romneys have enjoyed against those of (for example) divorced or single-mother households (even ones with similar financial resources), it would not be unreasonable to conclude that maybe living like the Romneys is a better idea than living like Rihanna and Chris Brown. If moral traditionalists are confident in their model of the good life—and, again, I think the evidence suggests that there is some reason for them to be—then the value of the institutions they prefer should be revealed by the free society rather than obscured by it. Likewise, the political model of marriage and family life probably obscures those values, for instance by making no-fault divorce the one-size-fits-all law of the land rather than making room for more traditional and binding models of marriage.

Such a broadening of the freedom of conscience would of course require buy-in from both sides of the culture-war skirmish lines. If we really want to take marriage private, then we must recognize, for example, the right of an Orthodox Jewish employer to decline to recognize same-sex marriages when developing employee benefits plans. Under such a regime, he might be pressured or shamed into offering equal treatment to same-sex couples, but he could not be sued or otherwise compelled to do so. People will get their feelings hurt in a free society, to be sure, but the best social technology we have for resolving such disputes is to recognize the value in others' preferences just as we would expect them to recognize the value in ours—not to agree, but to recognize the importance that others attach to their preferences. In Americans, this pushes all sorts of buttons related to the word *discrimination*, but such concerns are overblown. The situation that prevailed with African-Americans through the 1960s was unique and had been enforced at the point of guns and bayonets for hundreds of years. As the recent kerfuffle over Chick-fil-A's political activism suggests, gay Americans are not powerless victims in need of being rescued by political authorities.

The End Is Near

Look on every exit as being an entrance somewhere else.

—TOM STOPPARD, *ROSENCRANTZ AND GUILDENSTERN ARE DEAD*

The fiscal realities in the United States mean that very soon we will be forced to deal with a deep retrenchment in our expectations about what government can do for us. But as we have seen, whether the question is education, providing for health care, funding pensions, or providing for the poor, this presents us with many opportunities to make the world a much better place—for everybody. It will by no means be perfect—you should always fear and shun the utopian—but if we build the right kinds of institutions and allow innovation and investment to operate freely, we can make things better. We should do so not out of some kind of adolescent philosophy of absolute self-interest but by bearing in mind T. S. Eliot's haunting question: "What is the meaning of this city? Do you huddle close together because you love each other?" The answer is not to maximize our consumption function—not that there's anything wrong with that, but there is much more to human social life.

I have spent most of this book talking about our beliefs about what government can and cannot do *for* us. But there is an important related issue: what government can do *to* us.

In his wonderfully humane book *The Lily: Evolution, Play, and the Power of a Free Society*, Daniel Cloud makes the following so-obvious-nobody-ever-quite-said-it observation about the role of ships in the ancient world: "Once you own a ship, you, like a honeybee, are wherever you are voluntarily. If you choose to, you can sail away. You're in a position to negotiate with the king. He may put you in a ghetto, but the joke is on him, because you can fly; he's the one that's rooted in one place like a shrub. In fact, if you can find such a crazy place, you can base yourself where there is no king, where everything is up for negotiation, someplace across the sea like Attica or America. Classical civilization as a whole died a very long and gruesome physical death once there was no longer any place you could sail to if you wanted to get away from Caesar." At its apex—which is just about now—the realm of politics is very much like the world-girding empire Augustus inherited. We even call our most unaccountable government functionaries *czars*, which is a corruption of the word *Caesar*. There are some places you can go—the penumbras of the shadow banking system, the cash economy, or small, narrow-purpose safe havens—but for the broadly law-abiding middle class in the early years of this century, Caesar is everywhere.

Politics, like a market, is a forum for negotiation, but one with a critical defect: You cannot say no. Imagine that you are choosing a cell phone service provider. You walk into an AT&T wireless outlet, look at the phones on offer, and look at the various rate plans. There is a remarkably unhelpful person behind the counter, but that is the industry standard, so you don't pay much attention. You scrutinize the phones, the plans, the options. You think about how much you text or how much you don't text, whether you want Internet connectivity through your phone or just a simple phone. And if you don't see something you like, you walk away as the remarkably unhelpful person behind the counter glares at you. You say, "No." (Perhaps you even say "No, thanks," depending on the intensity of the glaring.) You disco on down to Verizon, or Joe's Cellular, or wherever, and you repeat the process. And if you don't see something you like, you keep saying no. Perhaps you even make a counteroffer to Joe's: "I like your plan, Joe, but it's about ten bucks a month on the high side. How's about backing off on the price a little bit?" Maybe Joe says yes, maybe Joe says no. A deal either happens or it doesn't. But you cannot say no to the outcome of an election, and saying no to the law is a risky business indeed, though we do it more often than you might think.

Imagine that we used something like the political process for this instead. Rather than going to a couple of stores or shopping online for the best deal, everybody in the country gets together and decides who is going to have which phone and what plan. Or, worse, everybody gets together and decides on *one* plan for everybody. The cellular companies would of course be keenly interested in the outcome of that process, and you could be sure that their influence would be felt in the corridors of cellular power. Maybe you'd wanted a bare-bones just-telephony plan, but you get stuck with the ninety-nine-dollars-a-month full-on plan—or maybe you'd wanted the full-on but the majority opts for the el cheapo. (Also, maybe you didn't want a cell phone at all, but we now have a national cell phone mandate—it worked for the insurance guys!) With the true classical public goods, you might make an argument that there is a good reason for us all to have the same plan: the same national security plan, the same law enforcement plan, the same federal highway network. (Bear in mind that this is no guarantee that it is going to be a *good* plan—consider the ugly and expensive mess that is the Interstate Highway System, the Spanish-American War, the War on Drugs, the Department of Homeland Security, etc.) But what would be the case for insisting that everybody have the same cell phone plan? And what would be the consequences?

Gordon Gekko's gigantic Reagan-era Motorola brick cost about $10,000 in current dollars, cost nearly $1,000 a month to operate, had very little talk time, needed its own purpose-built briefcase—and you couldn't play Angry Birds on it. At the time, it was a bigger deal than owning a Porsche, and now you couldn't give it away. (Literally: The giveaway phones available today are much better than was Gordon Gekko's top-of-the-line model.) Think about that for a second: The 1980s weren't that long ago, and, in at least one market (but there are many more), poor people today have much better stuff than rich people did a few decades ago. In fact, it would take very little for the twenty-first-century American to replicate the standard of living in the alleged golden age of the 1950s—the median income was only $10,000 a year in today's dollars, meaning that a full-time job at the minimum wage today (with two weeks off every year) would produce an income in excess of the typical household income in the 1950s, with some important exceptions—the worst new car for sale in the United States in 2012 is better than the best new car that was for sale in the United States in 1950; it is a technological marvel beyond mid-century dreams. Food, clothing, medical devices, and communication equipment have advanced beyond what even a Rockefeller could have had in the 1950s. How did that happen with cell phones, and why didn't it happen with education or health insurance?

What happened was that people began to say no to the Motorola cinder block. Motorola's competitors got a whiff of the fat profits the company was making from its mobile phones, and they got into the game. Some offered cell phones that were slightly less expensive, and some offered cell phones that were slightly better—sleeker, more talk time, etc. Motorola did not like being told no, and so it improved its products and prices. If you visit Retro Brick, a website for aficionados of vintage mobile phones (seriously—these people *exist*) you can watch electronics evolution scene by scene, like the cross section of a fossil index, beginning with the ur-mobile: "The 4500x and 4800x hand-portable or 'transportable' phones were mobile . . . just. Imagine a car battery with a car phone handset nailed to the top." There was no dramatic moment when cell phones went from being expensive and cumbrous to being cheap and tiny (and much more useful)—there was iteration after iteration, experiment after experiment, no after no after no. (Oddly enough, nobody's feelings seemed to be hurt by all this rejection.) By the 1990s, Motorola had introduced the tiny StarTAC phone—advertised as being the first "wearable" mobile phone—while Nokia had created the first popular smartphone, the Communicator 9000i. A decade later, we had the iPhone.

The right to say no is what political theorists call the right of Exit. An Exit-based system simply means that nobody can be coerced into any arrangement with anybody else. We would never accept somebody's ordering us around on something relatively trivial, like what kind of shampoo to buy, much less on something very important, like whom to marry. We insist on a right of Exit in all those relationships. Why do we accept that a small panel of mediocrities, mostly lawyers, in Washington can tell us what we have to do when it comes to so many things?

The cell phone's radical evolutionary improvement happened only because people had the right to walk away from devices and service providers that did not satisfy them. It seems an obvious point, but it is one that is often overlooked and misunderstood. We talk about technological progress as though Moore's law were an immutable law of thermodynamics, as though technological development *just happened*, a force of nature like a flood or a tadpole becoming a frog. But that is not the case. If you make a chart of the world's per capita GDP from A.D. 1 until now, you will see a flat line that lasts for the better part of two thousand years. And then the line goes vertical around 1750. "For the first time in history," writes economist Robert Lucas, "the living standards of the masses of ordinary people have begun to undergo sustained growth. . . . Nothing remotely like this economic behavior has happened before." Something changed in a few years, and it wasn't the people. It's not like we were monkeys in 1749 and Ben Franklins in 1750. All of the ingredients of the Industrial Revolution had been in place for years. We already knew how to make iron, build machines, and burn coal, and we'd been printing books with movable type since the fifteenth century, so such knowledge as there was could be distributed. Trade played a role, but there had been global trade for centuries before that.

The main change was that English people won the right to say no, and what they said no to largely was a lifetime of farmwork. They exercised a literal right of Exit, leaving the farms for the factories and the cities, or even for the colonies or the frontier. A two-thousand-year period of economic stagnation was broken in a matter of years, and the world was changed. We can do that again.

The power of Exit does not come only from political or contractual arrangements. It can come from informal social norms, and even from hard physical factors such as geography. The economist Arnold Kling argues that what kept the United States so remarkably free in its early days was not the presence of the Bill of Rights, but the presence of the frontier. The energetic, entrepreneurial people most likely to bridle at political restrictions had an out: lighting out for the territories. But what about Exit-oriented arrangements that do not require us to uproot ourselves and our lives to live in the wilderness? It is, in a real sense, possible to have a frontier within. Recalling Daniel Cloud's observations about the ancient world, Kling writes:

> I sometimes think that what kept the U.S. government small in the early 19th century was not so much the Constitution as the fact that people kept leaving the then-current United States for adjacent territories. The option to exit would have made it quite difficult for government to grow large and intrusive.
>
> But is there such a thing as too much right to exit? For example, suppose that I live on a street where we all share the same snow-removal service. When I see what we are going to be charged for a big storm, I opt out, so that I do not have to pay for snow removal. The street in front of my house goes unplowed, so that everyone else on the street is either blocked or has to pay more to get my part of the street plowed. Is that a good system?
>
> I do not think that this is an insoluble problem. In the private sector, there are situations where one consumer's exit can raise average costs. The solution is some form of lock-in. For example, condominium associations lock consumers into paying dues. Cell phone companies lock you into paying for a year or more of service.
>
> We allow private firms to implement lock-in policies, as long as they are reasonable. Similarly, I think we should allow physical or virtual communities that perform what we

now think of as government functions to implement lock-in policies as long as they are reasonable. I think we would need courts and an accumulation of common-law precedents to serve as the ultimate arbiter of when lock-in policies are reasonable and when they infringe on the right of exit.

Imagine that we had such a system in place today. My services for local police, fire, garbage collection, and snow removal have a lock-in arrangement that consists of me paying local property and sales taxes or going to jail. Perhaps the lock-in arrangement does not have to be that strong. Perhaps I could choose different service providers, either as an individual household or in conjunction with other households.

Call the incumbent service provider MoCo, and suppose that there are competing service providers that are specialists. I might want to keep MoCo's fire, police, and snow removal service, but instead get garbage collection from a separate trash hauler. What lock-in policies for MoCo are fair? It might be fair for them to offer discounts on garbage collection to people who already are consumers of other services. But it is not fair for them to deny a business license to the competing trash hauler.

I think that finding the balance between the right of exit and the legitimate use of lock-in policies should be done on a trial-and-error, case-by-case basis. . . . Once you start imagining competitive government, you can see that the right to exit is not as much of a threat as might appear to be the case at first.

There would of course be a great deal of disagreement about what constitutes "reasonable" in the above context. But there is no revolution without evolution, and the genius of the Anglo-American experiment in the eighteenth century was not merely imposing a system of enlightened governance on consenting populations (and giving them the option of lighting out for the territories if they didn't like it) but to allow an Exit-based ecosystem of social evolution to emerge on its own, in its own time, and under its own form. This was hardly limited to market-based, for-profit economic activity. The emergence of formal recognition of freedom of speech, freedom of the press, and freedom of religion was not the consequence of ruling elites finally seeing the light and embracing the wisdom of the great Johns—Locke, Mill, and Milton—but of their finally learning the hard way (the only way they learn) that having government police the podium, the press, and the pulpit does not work. In 1558, Queen Elizabeth gave England the Act of Uniformity, which mandated weekly church attendance at government-approved congregations using the Book of Common Prayer—because it was unthinkable that society could survive in peace if the people were left on their own to choose when, where, and if they would worship. By historical standards, it was only the blink of an eye later that George Mason, author of the Virginia Bill of Rights, made it clear that it was unthinkable that society could survive in peace if people were *not* left on their own to choose when, where, and if they would worship. Freedom of speech, freedom of the press, and freedom of religion have had their downsides, it is true: According to *USA Today*, the ten bestselling books of the past fifteen years were *Dr. Atkins' New Diet Revolution*, *The Da Vinci Code*, *Who Moved My Cheese?*, and seven Harry Potter novels, and there is just no excusing that, or the fact that the bestselling book of poetry in recent memory was written by the treacly songstress Jewel, or the evangelical persistence of whatever is your least favorite religious group—but there have been some upsides, too, for example, a notable lack of religious civil wars in the free world, the emergence of the Internet, the fact that you don't need anybody's permission to read the book you are holding, etc. Those who would argue today that we must have a single standard of education, a single standard of health insurance, or even a single standard for settling legal disputes are making precisely the same error Queen Elizabeth made, and in no small part for the same reasons: Politics doesn't trust people. Exit-based approaches by no means produce perfect results. People will join the Branch Davidians and lay out good money to read Jewel's gauzy poesy, but they also are free to become smarter and better, thereby making us as a society smarter and better in the aggregate. Some people will watch the Kardashians; some will watch iTunes U.

We know from experience that having government in charge of the press or our speech or our beliefs does not produce great literature, great thought, or great faith—it doesn't even produce versions of those things superior to what we come up with when left to our own devices. Leaving people to make their own decisions under their own standards means you get T. S. Eliot *and* Larry Flynt, while putting politics in charge means you get the National Endowment for the Arts and *People's Daily* . . . and the guillotine.

If we think of Mill's Harm Principle (summarized in the popular proverb as "Your right to swing your fist ends where my nose begins") and voluntary cooperation as pieces of social technology, then we can extend the metaphor and think of Exit as the algorithm at the heart of that software, the kernel that makes the whole thing work. Likewise, if we think of the science-inspired principle of humility as part of this infrastructure of social technology, it is sensible to conclude that we should set the bar for overruling Exit decisions quite high: Are you so sure that your preferred model of education or health care is the right one? So sure that you'd be willing to stick a gun in somebody's face over the issue? And if you're not sure you'd be willing to stick a gun in somebody's face over the issue, are you so sure that you'd be willing to pay somebody to stick a gun in somebody's face over the issue on your behalf? It is a little known irony of history that the practice of withholding income taxes from Americans' paychecks was dreamed up by an obscure economist in the Roosevelt administration by the name of Milton Friedman, who would later become a trenchant critic of the government overreach enabled by his policy innovation. Friedman, to his credit, always defended withholding as a necessary measure at that particular time and place—defeating Hitler and his totalitarian Axis co-conspirators was a pretty important piece of business, and given a choice between violating ideological niceties and allowing a pack of genocidal gangsters to run free across the globe, the choice was obvious. But few if any of our current political disputes rise to that level of seriousness. And the time is upon us to start making distinctions.

The power of government to coerce is challenged by mobility, affluence, and technology. Englishmen who were unhappy with the king could light out for America, just as some Americans today have decided to light out for Singapore or Dubai—or the black market. The federal government is working hard to suffocate the rise of innovations such as private currencies and powerful privacy technologies, but it is less and less able to do so every year—it can't even keep its own secrets. The federal government has been reduced to a thrashing and infantile thing, and the violence implicit in the system has risen to the surface. Consider the case of Anwar al-Awlaki, a U.S. citizen and al-Qaeda sympathizer denounced as "the Osama bin Laden of the Internet." He was a bilious Web propagandist and a favorite speaker on the jihad circuit. He was a loathsome man, to be sure, but there is a big difference between being the Osama bin Laden of the Internet and being Osama bin Laden. Not only did the U.S. government kill al-Awlaki without legal sanction and judicial process; the Obama administration had the audacity to announce its intention to assassinate a U.S. citizen—for *blogging*—in the pages of the *New York Times*. The administration also confirmed that it has a number of other U.S. citizens on its hit list. If that fact does not make you cynical about politics, then nothing will. (And I am surprised you have read this far.)

The unaddressed question here is, Is coercion even necessary? Or, more accurately, Is it necessary to invest a single social entity with the power to engage in coercion?

The case for a monopoly on violence is remarkably weak. As we saw in the case of the Wild West and the private security firms, competing organizations can and do provide security and dispute resolution services, and have in the past provided a measure of justice as well.

Short of your Hitlers and psychopathic killers, there are some very good alternatives to coercion. In a world of instantaneous information exchanges and complex social relationships, reputation is extraordinarily important. We should be looking at ways to use technology to build on that—something a little more sophisticated than Yelp reviews.

Here is a scenario that could easily play out in the next few years. Having decided to do something more profitable with your life than write books about politics, you have earned a great deal of money and decide to buy yourself a swanky sports car, a Superspeed Twin-Turbo, with a price tag of $85,000. You test-drive it, haggle a bit over the options, change your mind three times about the color, but finally come to a decision. You're going to finance it but decide to put $10,000 down, and so you hand the very pleased salesman your Bank of Singapore debit card (Bank of Singapore *of course*—good privacy standards). The salesman runs the card, and the commission-anticipating smile melts from his face. He hands you back the card with an apologetic "I'm sorry, there's a problem with your card." You: "My card has been declined?" SALESMAN: "No, your card has . . . declined *us*." A second later your iPhone buzzes with a text message: "This is an account alert from BeCool Card Services regarding your Bank of Singapore debit card. The Superspeed Twin-Turbo comes standard with tires manufactured by General Tire and Rubber (GTR), a wholly-owned subsidiary of GTR Global. In 2011, GTR Global set up four rubber plantations in Liberia on sites that were seized by the government after the military was deployed to drive indigenous people off of their land with no compensation. In accordance with your account preferences, which specify sanctions on companies engaged in exploitative or abusive practices in Africa, we are declining this transaction. If you have questions or concerns, please send a return text to this address and a customer-service representative will be in touch within 30 minutes. Thank you for using BeCool, and thank you for being cool." You think for a second about your BeCool account, which is attached to your debit card and your main credit card, and which you have instructed to block certain kinds of transactions with companies engaged in activities or business practices you find distasteful or unethical. At the top of your list are companies that use cozy relationships with governments in poor and undeveloped countries to exploit local populations. Every now and again, BeCool stops a transaction: for a pair of shoes sewn by prison laborers in China, a tank of gas from Citgo, which is affiliated with the Hugo Chavez government in Venezuela. It's been little things so far, never something as big as a car. You could always use a different card or go to the bank to get a cashier's check—you want the car, but you really don't want to think about poor Liberians every time you drive it, either.

While you are deliberating, Superspeed gets an email from Be-Cool, alerting them that a transaction has been blocked because of GTR's dubious practices in Liberia. This is the 211th email about those tires that Superspeed has received in the past eighteen months. Superspeed sells 50,000 cars a year, so 211 lost sales is not a catastrophic event—but that does amount to almost $18 million in lost business. The vice president for marketing is starting to get a little nervous about it, and has logistics look into what it would cost to replace GTR tires with a similar high-quality product. Phone calls are made.

A week later, you get another text message from BeCool: "This is an account alert from BeCool Card Services. We are writing to inform you that Superspeed Inc. has informed us of their intention to replace the GTR tires on all future models with products that meet our ethical standards. Following Superspeed's announcement, BiTurbo Inc. and Halloway Heavy Equipment both announced plans to sever ties with GTR. Thanks again for being cool."

And you go buy the car with a clear conscience.

When it comes to organizing community life, coercion is not the only tool in the toolbox: We have negotiation, commerce, voluntary association, and—often overlooked—the power of reputation. The main problem with reputation networks is that historically they have favored the interests of large, well-established organizations over those of individuals and small groups, largely as a consequence of economies of scale. Technology and social innovation give us an opportunity to change that in important and productive ways.

The most powerful reputation network that most of us are familiar with is the credit-rating system. In the United States, as in most advanced countries, we do not have debtors' prisons, and in fact the ability of banks and other businesses to collect on debts is quite limited. You can walk away from a mortgage and, while the bank may be able to foreclose on your house, it is nearly impossible for the bank to force you to pay off the mortgage, even if the house is worth less than you owe on it (an unhappily common circumstance of late). In some states, the bank cannot even take the house under most circumstances. You can walk into an Apple store, finance $10,000 worth of top-of-the-line gear, go home, and refuse to make a single payment—and in most jurisdictions, Apple cannot even come to your house and take the stuff back. You can put $10,000 worth of fine Scotch and lap dances on your American Express card, refuse to pay, and American Express has relatively few options to force you to do so. What American Express can do is cut off your credit, refuse to lend you any more money, and—most important— let everybody else know that you are somebody who refuses to pay his debts. American Express may never get its $10,000 back, but it can sure as hell inflict $50,000 worth of inconvenience on you, and maybe a lot more.

An interesting thing about the credit-reporting system: Even the most ruthless competitors cooperate with each other. You would think that American Express would have very strong incentives to keep your misdeeds to itself: Why would it go out of its way to help Visa, MasterCard, or any of its other competitors? A narrowly, rationally self-interested American Express would hope that Visa would be dumb enough to give you a $10,000 line of credit. Bank X does not stand to gain by warning Bank Y and Bank Z about bad credit risks, yet doing so is a standard and essential part of doing business in a modern economy. And as anybody who has ever had bad credit knows, reputation is an asset with real value, and damage to one's reputation can impose real costs. Travel has become virtually impossible without a credit card. Try buying airline tickets, checking into a hotel, or renting a car without a major credit card: It can be done, but it is difficult. Buying a house, renting an apartment, and getting certain kinds of jobs can be impossible with bad credit. The difference between excellent credit and poor credit can mean thousands of dollars when buying a car or making another high-end purchase.

But most of our reputation networks are very top-down and hierarchical. It is true that businesses have to worry about their credit ratings, too, but only vis-à-vis bigger and more powerful businesses, mostly banks and institutional investors. For individuals, the credit-reporting system can at times feel stacked against the little guy—a false report that damages one's credit can be contested and repaired, but it is a difficult and cumbrous process, and the chances of being compensated for a false report are remote.

At the other end of the spectrum are bottom-up reputation networks, which abound on the Internet. Customer reviews on sites such as Yelp, Amazon, and Expedia shift the balance of power from the large enterprises to the individual consumer. I have friends who simply will not rent a movie (over Apple TV, naturally) if it has a low score on Rotten Tomatoes. There are wildly different levels of credibility in bottom-up reputation networks, and the structure of the network is important. There are a lot of reputation vandals on Wikipedia, for example (as anybody involved in politics can tell you), but the Wikipedia community is robust and responsive enough to minimize the impact of professional slanderers. There are similar vandals among Amazon book reviewers, but the Amazon community has developed a sophisticated understanding of the book review ecosystem, in essence developing an informal reputation network for those who participate in its reputation network, with some reviewers being very trusted and some being obvious cranks. There are very thoughtful critics on Yelp who develop followings of their own, just as there are professional movie critics who are trusted and those who are not. There has been a good deal of scholarly attention paid to the question of online reputation networks, indicating that while there are both vandals and self-servers (businesses that pose as consumers and review their own businesses), there is a remarkable level of consistency, which is indicative of honesty and reliability. Rotten Tomatoes is not perfect, but then neither is the *New York Times* movie section.

What is needed is a good model for highly sophisticated, reliable, transparent, bottom-up reputation networks, which probably would differ from online review communities in important ways. Rather than being strictly crowdsourced, they would need to be professionally administered, especially if they are dealing with issues more consequential than the quality of the appetizers at a trendy restaurant. Some of those could be strictly fact-based—a company donates money to Candidate X or Cause Y—but the more important thing is that they be actionable. Right now, I can go to OpenSecrets.org or the Federal Election Commission website and find out who is supporting which candidates, what lobbying organizations, what political-action committees. What is needed is the next step—for instance, indexing companies according to consumer-specified values profiles and linking that information with point-of-purchase technology, as in the imaginary BeCool example above. Boycotts and other consumer action can be powerful tools for shaping behavior—the Montgomery Bus Boycott being the gold standard—but boycotts, like most other political action, are stuck in the nineteenth century. Think of the Chick-fil-A dispute. Other than the fact that the word was spread on social media, the Chick-fil-A boycott/antiboycott could have played out in more or less the same way sixty years ago: People hear about a situation from a media organization, spread the word, and then stage protests, counterprotests, letter-writing campaigns, etc. Imagine if there were a real-world service like BeCool, and 100,000 people had specified that they did not wish to do business with a firm that opposed gay marriage (or a firm that supported gay marriage, for that matter). If Chick-fil-A found itself on the wrong side of the naughty-or-nice list, it could do the math itself and decide whether its political interests were sufficiently aligned with its business interests. If Starbucks were to learn that 100,000 people (not an unreasonable number out of a country of 300 million) had decided not to do business with it for one reason or another, its executives could pretty quickly calculate that they were forgoing between a few hundred thousand and a few million dollars a week in sales.

In a sense, this model of action is more democratic than traditional political processes, which in most cases fail to account for the intensity of preferences. I care about a great many issues, but some I care about intensely, and a few I care about so intensely that I would choose not to do business with firms on the other side of the issue and might go out of my way to do business with firms on the right side of the issue. There are people who care about gay marriage, but do not care very much about it, and then there are people who care very intensely about it. In an election, everybody's vote carries the same value; in a reputation-network model, people have the opportunity to account for the intensity of their feelings, and firms have the opportunity to respond to it. The arrangement itself is value-neutral—pro-life groups have the same power of influence as pro-choice groups—but the intellectual architecture of the system would be far more sophisticated than most of what is available through consumer action.

When the Chick-fil-A fight was in the news—and someday, future archeologists will be puzzled by the cultural connection between sex and chicken sandwiches in the early twenty-first century—it was complicated by political intrusion. The mayors of Chicago, Boston, and San Francisco all threatened to use their official powers to impede Chick-fil-A's business operations in their cities. There were many who opposed Chick-fil-A's position and supported gay marriage who nonetheless thought this improper. It is one thing for consumers to refuse to patronize a business with repellent values, but another for elected officials to use governmental powers to punish people who hold contrary political views. Rob Halford, the leather-clad gay stereotype who fronts the deathless heavy-metal band Judas Priest, showed himself to be a true Englishman when he channeled John Milton and *Areopagitica* when interviewed about the dispute. The company has its point of view, the boycotters have their point of view, and the anti-boycotters have their point of view, and, as Halford argued, the real value of living in a free society is that those points of view can peaceably contest for dominance in the public marketplace of ideas, and that the best ideas, like the best products, eventually will prevail. "The supporters have been showing up in droves, to spend money at the restaurants and peacefully assemble," he said. "But there has obviously been so many people who have gone out and boycotted the company. I think it's great. That's our right here. What you're seeing here are the elements of the American Constitution in all of their glory." It is indicative of our political culture that British heavy-metal icons understand the foundations of the American order better than the mayors of Boston, San Francisco, or Chicago—and the mayor of Chicago was in his previous job the White House chief of staff. In the same interview, Halford charmingly described the affection he had developed for the American founders while watching a documentary about John Adams. Compared with the elected mayors, he sounded like Thomas Jefferson.

Under preference-respecting social norms, it is a significant social problem when the mayor of Chicago threatens to use government to punish private citizens for their political beliefs—but it is no problem at all for private citizens to decline to associate with others for the same reason. One of the most powerful tools the self-government wagon trains of the frontier era had for enforcing norms was "neighboring." Neighboring was the process by which individuals in the wagon train shared essential goods during the journey and engaged in the exchange of goods and the division of labor. One of the possible sanctions spelled out in wagon train by-laws was the refusal to neighbor with people who did not follow the rules. This was a powerful disincentive for antisocial behavior: It was a long, thirsty, hungry, dangerous way across the prairie. Imagine an extreme version of that in modern society. Through purely voluntary, noncoercive action—declining to buy from or sell to an offender—we could enforce social norms with no violence at all. Maybe we wouldn't put you in prison, but we could instantly reduce you to a standard of living well below the average North Korean's, or Robinson Crusoe's, for that matter.

This is an enormously powerful social tool, and one with deep evolutionary roots. For lower primates and less advanced human societies, to be excluded from the social group is something very close to a death sentence. The relative affluence and specialization of complex societies have somewhat attenuated the power of alienation, which is probably a good thing. There are not very many political opinions over which I want to send somebody to starve in the wilderness. But a corporate death sentence is a very different thing. A preference for voluntary, market-based institutions is not the same thing as faith in the good intentions of corporations, business executives, or anybody else. Businesses engage in unethical shenanigans all the time, and those with a very powerful incentive to monitor such things already do a pretty good job of it through market institutions. When Enron hit the fan, it was news to everybody except investors in the firm. Long before the credit-rating agencies downgraded its debt, and long before regulators and law enforcement agencies uncovered evidence of its malfeasance, Enron had lost more than 80 percent of its value on the stock market, which is a very powerful reputation network.

What is needed is not a Standard and Poor's for business ethics, but hundreds of Standard and Poor's for all sorts of values, a *Consumer Reports* with some real technological teeth in it or a Better Business Bureau that can cost you a billion bucks for being bad. Consider that in the United States and England in the nineteenth century, there were few if any laws against cannibalism or incest. Those acts were so close to being unthinkable that nobody thought to pass a law against them—it just went without saying. Google's informal corporate motto—Don't Be Evil—should be one of those things that should go without saying, too, in every boardroom in the country, but it doesn't.

We have the power to say no. If one-tenth of us refused to pay our taxes next year, the government would have neither a sufficient number of agents to arrest us nor sufficient jail cells to incarcerate us nor enough courts to try us. And the day will come when we do have to say no. And now is the time to think very carefully about what we—all of us, in this together—are going to say yes to.

ACKNOWLEDGMENTS

The two critical resources when writing a book are time and inspiration, both of which have been provided to me by two friends and colleagues to whom I am deeply grateful: *National Review* editor Rich Lowry and *National Review* publisher Jack Fowler. My cherished friends and colleagues Jay Nordlinger and Jason Lee Steorts have been endlessly helpful to me in my endeavors to become less wrong over time, and any errors herein are properly understood as my failure to learn rather than their failure to teach. (And for the very useful phrase *less wrong*, I am indebted to the work of Eliezer Yudkowsky.) I would in fact be bereft without the extended *National Review* family.

I thank Natasha Simons for her semiheroic endurance of my habit of developing this thesis out loud and in what must have been excruciating detail after too much coffee. To Roger Kimball I am grateful for his irreplaceable friendship. John Podhoretz, Jonah Goldberg, and Glenn Beck all have treated me with great generosity at no possible gain to themselves.

Adam Bellow and his associates at HarperCollins, abetted by my agent, Matthew Carnicelli, have labored manfully to bring out the best in my work, and I am grateful to them all. I would like to assure them that I am not part of a conspiracy to increase the sales of Prinivil.

My friends at the Institute for Humane Studies have provided critical intellectual guidance, great heaping reams of invaluable reading material, and, at a moment when it was very much needed, a job at their unique organization, which allowed me one of the most productive years of reading and listening in my life, a direct result of which is this book.

INDEX

Index

Index

ABOUT THE AUTHOR

KEVIN D. WILLIAMSON covers politics, economics, and culture for *National Review*. He began his journalism career at the Bombay-based Indian Express Newspaper Group, and his work has appeared in the *New York Post*, the *New York Daily News*, *Commentary*, the *New Criterion*, *Academic Questions*, *The Daily*, and other publications. He is a regular commentator on Fox News, CNBC, and talk radio. He is a native of West Texas and lives in New York City.

DATE DUE

MAY - - 2013